Mapping Alberta's Political Leadership:

A Comprehensive Account of Edmonton's

MLAs from 1905-2003

By the same authors

By Austin Mardon A Conspectus of the Contribution of Herodotus to the Development of Geographical Thought 1990;
International Law and Space Rescue Systems 1991;
Kensington Stone and Other Essays 1991;
A Transient in Whirl 1991;
Alone Against the Revolution 1996;
Political Networks in Alberta 1905-1992 2002;
7 days in Moscow 2005;
The Contribution of Geography to the Recovery of Antarctic Meteorites 2005;

By Ernest Mardon Narrative Unity of the Cursor Mundi 1967;
The Founding Faculty of the University of Lethbridge 1968;
Place Names of Southern Alberta 1970;
The Conflict Between the Individual & Society in the Plays of James Bridie 1971;
Who's Who in Federal Politics from Alberta Ridings 1972;
English Studies at Canadian Universities 1972;
Community Names of Alberta 1975

By Austin Mardon & Ernest Mardon
Alberta Judicial Biographical Dictionary 1990;
Alberta Ethnic Mormon Politicians 1991;
Alberta Ethnic German Politicians 1991;
When Kitty Met the Ghost 1991;
Down & Out & On the Run in Moscow 1991;
The Girl Who Could Walk Through Walls 1991;
Alberta Mormon Politicians 1992;
Alberta General Election Returns & Subsequent Byelections 1882-1992 1993;
Edmonton Political Biography 1994;
Alberta Political Biographical Dictionary 1994;
Alberta Executive Council 1905-1990 1994;
Early Christian Saints 1997;
Later Christian Saints for Children 1997;
Many Christian Saints for Children 1997;
Childhood Memories & Legends of Christmas Past 1998;
Community Names of Alberta 1999;
Men of Dawn 1999;
United Farmers of Alberta 1999;
The Genealogy of the Mardon Family 2000;
Alberta Catholic Politicians 2000; Alberta Anglican Politicians 2001;
Liberal Politicians in Alberta 1905-1992 2002;
What's in a Name? 2002;
Edmonton Members of the Legislature 2004;
Senators and Members of the House of Commons from Edmonton
Edmonton Municipal Politicians 2005;
Alberta Francophone Politicians 2007.

POLITICAL LEADERSHIP:

A Comprehensive Account of Edmonton's

MLAs from 1905-2003

By Ernest G. Mardon, Austin A. Mardon, & Joseph Harry Veres

Edited by Justin Selner

Edmonton, Alberta, Canada

2011

A Golden Meteorite Press Book.

Cover Artwork: Lawrence Dommer, 2011

Published by Golden Meteorite Press.
126 Kingsway Garden
Post Office Box 34181
Edmonton, Alberta
T5G 3G4
Canada

Library and Archives Canada Cataloguing in Publication

Mapping Alberta's political leadership : a comprehensive account of Edmonton's MLAs from 1905-2003 / Ernest G. Mardon ... [et al.].

ISBN 978-1-897472-30-9

1. Politicians--Alberta--Edmonton--Biography.
2. Edmonton (Alta.)--Politics and government--20th century--Biography. I. Mardon, Ernest G., 1928-

FC3696.25.M448 2011 971.23009'9 C2011-904815-9

Dedicated To May G. Knowler

Acknowledgements

Any study of this sort is dependent upon the support and efforts of a wide variety of people. The authors would like to thank the staff at the Provincial Archives of Alberta, the Legislative Library of Alberta, the University of Alberta, the University of Calgary, the Calgary Public Library, the Edmonton Public Library, and last but not least, the Lethbridge Public Library, for all of their assistance and encouragement. They would also like to thank staff of the Historical Site and Archive Service, Alberta Community Development, including Carl Betke, Les Hurt, and Michael Payne, for their help in preparing this manuscript for publication and for their support of the project. Finally, the authors wish to thank Justin Selner for his editorial and literary skills. It should be noted that facts of this study may differ from other published work, and any errors or omissions remain the responsibility of the authors alone.

Table of Contents

Introduction

This study is intended to serve both as an aid to future research and as a reference source for individuals interested in the history of Edmonton. It brings information from a variety of sources including newspapers, arrival records, written historical works, and interviews together on the men and women who have made Edmonton from 1905 to the present. This monograph contains all Edmonton Member of the Alberta Legislature, from its creation by the Canadian Parliament into the twenty-first century. This is the result of intensive archival research. There has been no attempt made here to analyze the behavior of an individual or to provide a detailed account of an individual career before entering the Chamber, during their Membership in the Legislature, or throughout their subsequent career. It is primarily a reference book. One aspect of the political history of the province can be read in this study. If the reader desires a readable, brief, political history, the authors would recommend the late Ernest S. Watkins' The Golden Province (1980)

Although no attempt has been made here to analyze voting patterns and behaviours, or to provide a detailed narrative account of individual election campaigns, much of the political history of Alberta can be read in theses biographical profiles. For instance, the decline of Alberta's Liberal Party and the triumph of the United Farmers of Alberta are readily apparent in the results of the general election of June 1921. The subsequent tribulations of Premier Brownlee and the spectacular rise of William Aberhart can be traced in the massive victory of the Social Credit Party in the general election of August 1935. The general election of 1971 details yet another fundamental shift in the political landscape of Alberta as 36 years of Social Credit government gave way to a new Progressive Conservative government led by Premier Lougheed, then to Premier Getty, and finally to the present Premier, Ralph Klein.

In provincial elections, the single-member plurality voting system was used in the first election of 1905 and then not again until 1959. Since

1959 Alberta has returned to single member constituencies. Certain variations from this prescription are as noted: In 1909 both Edmonton and Calgary elected two representatives each in recognition of their population size and individual electors were allowed to cast two ballots. In 1913 only Edmonton remained as a two-member constituency, but in 1917 two unusual variations were introduced. First, sitting members in service with the armed forces were not required to defend their seats and were thus automatically returned to the Legislature. Second, nurses and members of the armed forces were allowed to vote in a province-wide ballot for two special Representatives over and above the regular provincial constituency representatives. In 1921 Edmonton and Calgary both elected 5 members and Medicine Hat 2 members. Voters in these constituencies could cast as many ballots as there were members to be elected, and these representatives were chosen on the basis on the highest vote totals.

Between the 1924 Edmonton by-election and 1955 provincial general elections, Alberta adopted a relatively complex and unusual system of both preferential and proportional voting. All constituencies, except for Edmonton and Calgary, were single-member constituencies. In single-member ridings electors marked their ballots in order of preference. If no candidate received a majority of votes cast as the first preference of the electorate, the bottom candidate in the field was dropped and his or her votes were transferred to the other remaining candidates on the basis of marked second preferences. This process was continued until one candidate obtained a clear majority of votes cast. Edmonton and Calgary remained multi-member ridings and elected between 5 and 7 representatives depending upon the election year. Candidates in both Edmonton and Calgary campaigned on a citywide basis and were declared elected on the basis of a system of proportional representation.

Such systems of proportional and preferential balloting were relatively popular especially in Western Canada in the 1920's and 1930's. However, few other jurisdictions retained these methods of selecting representatives as long as Alberta did or applied them so broadly. Historians and political scientists generally agree that the popularity of both preferential and transferable ballots is connected to a widespread distrust in

Western Canada of the power of political parties. What is less clear is what effect, if any, these voting systems had on actual representation in provincial legislatures. In theory, at least, preferential ballots give an undue weight to the second and third choices of voters whose first choice ran last or next to last in the actual campaign. However, figures from Alberta elections would seem to indicate that the composition of the provincial legislature between 1940 and 1955 would have remained essentially the same had the province used a simple system of declaring the person with the plurality of the votes cast elected. In only 7 of 237 cases in this period was someone elected who was not leading on the first ballot.

The political history of Alberta is replete with colourful characters, stirring campaigns, and interesting experiments in both representation and political philosophy. If this study serves to encourage further research on Alberta's distinctive political culture or to interest ordinary Albertans in their political history it will have more than satisfied the aspirations of its authors.

Nevertheless, the historical facts and dates and general information never differ from other archival and published details. The authors take complete responsibility for any errors or omissions in the text.

"Though our sins may be scarlet, we hope our book will be read!"

Biographies:

"All history resolves itself very easily into the biography of a few stout and earnest persons."

Ralph Waldo Emerson (1803 -1882)

Edmonton

EDMONTON

• Capital city of the Province of Alberta

Lovell's “Gazetteer of British North America,” published in 1872, states that, "Edmonton is a fortified village in the Northwest Territories in Lat. 53 degrees 33' Long. 113 degrees 28' west. It is built of red earth, enclosed by high pickets, and entered by a battlemented gateway. Its vicinity is rich in coal and gold and other minerals". It took its name from Fort Edmonton, built in 1795, twenty miles farther down the North Saskatchewan River, by George Sutherland, of the Hudson's Bay Company. It was named after Edmonton, near London, England, probably as a compliment to John Prudens (Sutherland's clerk, who was born there). However, the Indians destroyed the fort in 1807. To compensate, a new fort of the same name was built in 1808 on the slope of the high bank within the limits of the present city of Edmonton. Later, the word "Fort" fell into disuse. When the first post office was opened on February 1, 1877, it was named simply, EDMONTON.

An Alphabetical List of Provincial Edmonton Politicians

Adams, Clayton

MEMBER OF THE LEGISLATURE 1948 -1952

Born January 9, 1882 in Summerside, P.E.I., son of Edward Adams and Margaret Baker. He was of United Empire Loyalist stock and a Lutheran. Educated at Summerside, Adams was the Chairman of the Industrial Relation Board of the provincial government. Clayton Adams was returned as a Social Credit member for the multi-member Edmonton Constituency. He sat in the Chamber as a government backbencher for four years. In 1952 he did not seek re-election and retired from politics at the age of seventy.

Source of information:

Canadian Parliamentary Guide (1950) p. 424

Canadian Parliamentary Guide (1952)

Alexander, Keith

MEMBER OF THE LEGISLATURE 1982 -1985

Born July 23, 1930 in Vulcan, Alberta, son of John R. Alexander and Theta LaVerne Vaugh. Educated in Calgary, Alexander attended the University of Colorado at Boulder, where he graduated in arts. He became an Edmonton businessman and the vice-president of Dominion Securities America. R. Keith Alexander was returned as the P.C. Member for Edmonton Whitemud in 1982. He sat as a government backbencher for three years. When Donald R. Getty was chosen the Alberta Progressive Conservative leader at the Edmonton convention in October 13, 1985, Alexander vacated his seat so the new premier could re-enter the Legislature.

Source of information:

Canadian Parliamentary Guide (1985) p. 670

Canadian Parliamentary Guide (1984)

Amerongen, Gerald Joseph

MEMBER OF THE LEGISLATURE 1971-1986

Born July 18, 1914 in Winnipeg, Manitoba, son of Maximilian W. E. Taets Von Amcrongen and his wife Maria Waas. He was of ethnic German descent and a Roman Catholic. His father was a prominent Edmonton businessman. Amerongen was educated in both Regina, Saskatoon and Edmonton, Alberta where he attended the University of Alberta, graduating in arts and then in law. While on campus, he served as the president of the Student's Union. He was admitted to the Alberta Bar in 1946 and was appointed to the Queen's Counsel in 1965. Gerry Amerongen became a prominent Edmonton Conservative Roman Catholic lawyer. He was an unsuccessful P. C. candidate in 1955, 1959, 1963, and 1967. However, in 1971, Amerongen was returned the Tory member for Edmonton Meadowlark and the next year he became the Speaker of the Legislature. He held this position for 14 years. In 1986 he was defeated by Liberal Grant Mitchell. Following his defeat, Amerongen then retired from politics at the age of seventy-two. In the 1999 Canadian Law List, Amerongen's name appears as a practicing lawyer.

Source of information: Canadian Parliamentary Guide (1985)

Canadian Law List (1999)

Canadian Parliamentary Guide (1972) p. 487

Ashton, John G.

Born March 31, 1935 in Hanna, Alberta, son of Norman John Ashton and Sophie Jane French. He is of ethnic English/Welsh descent and a Catholic. As a young man, Ashton served three years as an officer in the Royal Canadian Navy. He later attended the University of Alberta where he graduated in arts and then in law. He was admitted to the Alberta Bar in 1964 and became a lawyer in Sherwood Park. John G. Ashton was elected as the Progressive Conservative member for Edmonton Ottowell, where he sat in the Legislature for eight years. In 1979 he did not seek re-election and retired from politics at the age of forty-four. In 1984 he was made a Queen's Counselor.

Source of information:

Canadian Parliamentary Guide (1972) p. 487

Atkinson, William A.

MEMBER OF THE LEGISLATURE 1930-1935

Born May 18, 1876 in Buthrie, Ontario, son of Charles Greenwood Atkinson and Martha Hanna Turner. William Albert Atkinson was educated to qualify as a medical doctor. His father's parents had emigrated from Yorkshire, England in the early 19th century. As a young man, Atkinson settled in Edmonton where he became a prominent physician. He won election to the Provincial Legislature in the 1930 General election as one of the six members for the Edmonton Constituency. However, in the 1935 Provincial election he was defeated in the Edmonton riding

Source of information:

C. M. D. (1935)

Canadian Parliamentary Guide (1932)

Canadian Parliamentary Guide (1934) p. 334

Barner, S. A. Gordon

MEMBER OF THE LEGISLATURE 1935-1940

Born August 10, 1875 in Warwick, Ontario, son of Samuel David Barner and Lois Hagle. His mother was of United Empire Loyalist stock. Educated at Strathroy Collegiate Institute, he attended Toronto Normal School, qualifying as a schoolteacher. Barner came to Alberta and elected to reside in Edmonton. Here, he pursued a career as an instructor of mathematics and science at Alberta College in 1909. Later he became an Edmonton businessman in the insurance field. S. A. Gordon Barner served as an Edmonton Public School Trustee from 1911 to 1917, from 1920 to 1925, and from 1927 to 1936, accumulating a total of twenty years or service. S. A. Gordon Barner was returned as a Social Credit Member for the multi-member Edmonton Constituency in 1935 where he sat for five years in the Legislature. In 1940 he failed in his re-election bid as Progressive candidate.

Source of information:

Canadian Parliamentary Guide (1939)

Canadian Parliamentary Guide (1936) p. 378

Barrett, Pamela

MEMBER OF THE LEGISLATURE 1986-1993 and 1997-2001

Born November 26, 1953 in Brandon, Manitoba, daughter of Ray Barret and Agatha Terry. She is of Scottish descent and a

Roman Catholic. She attended the University of Alberta, graduating in arts and then Glasgow University, graduating with a Master's degree. After her formal education, Barrett became an Edmonton economic / politics researcher. Pam Barrett was returned the NDP member for Edmonton Highlands in 1986 and became her party's deputy leader for seven years. In 1993 she did not seek re-election. In 1997 Pam Barrett was again returned as the New Democratic Member for Edmonton Highlands and was now the party leader. However, in 2001 she did not seek re-election.

Source of information:

Canadian Parliamentary Guide (2002) p. 555

Canadian Parliamentary Guide (1988) p. 682

Canadian Parliamentary Guide (1999)

Beniuk, Andrew

MEMBER OF THE LEGISLATURE 1993-1997

Born April 26, 1994 in St. Paul, Alberta, son of John Beniuk and Katherine Wowk. He was of Ukrainian descent and a former commercial real estate agent. Andrew G. Beniuk was returned the Progressive Conservative Member for Edmonton Norwood in 1993 where he sat as a private member on the opposition side of the Chamber for four years. In 1997 he failed in his re-election bid, losing to Liberal Susan Olsen. He then retired from provincial politics at the age of fifty-five.

Source of information:

Canadian Parliamentary Guide (1995) p. 552

Betkowski, Nancy (nee Elliott)

[Also see Nancy MacBeth]

MEMBER OF THE LEGISLATURE 1986-1993 and 1997-2001

Born December 29, 1948 in Edmonton, Alberta, daughter of Dr. F. George Elliot and his wife Dorothy. Educated in Edmonton, Miss Elliott attended the University of Alberta, graduating in arts, and then proceeded to enroll at the University of Laval. She later became an executive assistant to Deputy Premier Dr. Hugh Homer. Nancy Betkowski was returned as the Progressive Conservative member for the Edmonton Glenora constituency in 1986. Upon her electoral victory, Premier Getty immediately appointed her to the Cabinet as the Minister of Education from 1986 to 1989. In 1989 Betkowski was named Minister of Health and by 1992 she was recognized as one of the ablest members of Premier Getty's cabinet. When Premier Getty retired as the Alberta Progressive Conservative leader in 1992, Ms. Betkowski placed second to Ralph Klein for the leadership of the party on the second vote. She did not seek re-election in the 1993 general election. In 1998 she had remarried to Hillard MacBeth. Betkowski then joined the Liberals and became the Alberta Liberal leader later that year. Nancy MacBeth successfully re-entered the Legislature when she was returned the Liberal Member in the June 1998 Edmonton McClung by-election. In the 2001 general election, Liberal Nancy MacBeth (nee Elliott) placed second losing to Tory Mark Norris.

Source of Information:

Canadian Parliamentary Guide (1983)

Canadian Parliamentary Guide (1968)

Blakeman, Laurie

MEMBER OF THE LEGISLATURE 1997-

Bom May 23, 1958 in Edmonton, daughter of Denis Blakeman and his wife Evelyn. She attended the University of Alberta, graduating in fine arts in 1980 and in public administration in 1990. Laurie Blakeman (Mrs. Ben Henderson) was returned as the Liberal Member for Edmonton Centre in 1997 and was again re-elected in 2001.

Source of information:

Canadian Parliamentary Guide (2002) p. 556

William 'Bill' Bonner

MEMBER OF THE LEGISLATURE 1997-

Born September 26, 1944. He attended the University of Alberta, graduating in physical education and then in education. Bonner became an Edmonton schoolteacher from 1977 to 1997. William 'Bill' Bonner was returned as the Liberal member for Edmonton Glengarry in 1997 and was re-elected in 2001.

Source of information:

Canadian Parliamentary Guide (2002) p. 556

Bowen, John Campbell

MEMBER OF THE LEGISLATURE 1921-1926

LIEUTENANT GOVERNOR 1937-1950

Born October 3, 1872 in Osgoode Township, Carleton County near Ottawa, son of Peter Bowen and Margaret Poast and brother of Peter E. Bowen. While his primary education was acquired in Ottawa, he later attended Brandon College in Manitoba, where he graduated with a theology degree. Bowen then held charges in Baptist churches at Chuphin and Winnipeg before being appointed secretary of the Board of Education for the Baptist Union of Western Canada. However, ill health forced his retirement from that post. Bowen then came to Alberta and settled in Edmonton, where he became the pastor of the Strathcona Baptist Church. In 1906 he married Edith Oliver, formerly of Blemhirnc, Ontario. They had two daughters, Ruth Brown, who was for years one of the editors of the Edmonton Journal, and Mrs. Margaret Neal of Edmonton. During World War I, John C. Bowen enlisted in the Canadian Army and served as an army chaplain on the Western Front with the rank of Colonel. On his demobilization, he returned to Edmonton where he was active in community affairs, serving as an Alderman for two years. Interested in Provincial politics, John Campbell Bowen, running as a Liberal, successfully contested the five-member Edmonton Constituency in 1921. He sat in the Legislature for five years as a private member on the opposition side of the House. For a time he was also the Liberal House Leader. However, in the 1926 election, Bowen failed in his re-election bid. Prime Minister MacKenzie King appointed John C. Bowen as the sixth Lieutenant Governor of the Province of Alberta on March 23, 1937 after the sudden death of Lt. Gov. P. C. H. Primrose while the Legislature was in session. Bowen drew national attention when only a few weeks later, he refused to give royal assent to three bills passed by the Legislature. He referred the bills, which sought to improve newspaper censorship, increase the tax on banks and regulate credit institution. All of them subsequently were ruled ultra vires of the Legislature by the Supreme Court of Canada. Bowen notably held the vise regal position for thirteen years (a record) and resigned in 1950 due to ailing health.

John Campbell Bowen died January 2, 1958 in Edmonton.

It should also be noted that J. C. Bowen was a successful Edmonton Aldermanic candidate in the 1920, 1921 and 1928 elections, and he was an unsuccessful Mayoral candidate in 1928.

Source of Information:

Canadian Parliamentary Guide

(1925)

Canadian Parliamentary Guide (1949)

Canadian Parliamentary Guide (1926) p. 531

Boyle, John R

ALDERMAN 1905

MEMBER OF THE LEGISLATURE 1905-1924

Born February 3, 1871 in Sykeston, near Samia, Ontario son of William and Annie Boyle. Educated in Sarnia, he then taught in the Lambton County Schools for three years. Coming to the Northwest Territories in 1894, he taught in Regina for some time before taking up the study of law. Boyle articled with MacKenzie and Brown of Regina before moving to Edmonton. He then completed his legal studies under Hedly C. Taylor and was called to the NWT Bar in 1899. He was later associated with the Edmonton law firm of Taylor, Boyle and Parlee; and after Taylor was appointed a judge in 1907, the firm simply became "Boyle and Parlee."

Politically, Boyle served as a City Alderman in 1904. John Robert Boyle also successfully ran as an Edmonton Aldermanic candidate in 1905 and 1906. He resigned in May 1906, on his being returned to the first Alberta Legislature. Interested in Provincial politics, J. R. Boyle running as a Liberal successfully contested Sturgeon in 1905. He sat in the Legislature for the next nineteen years. In 1906 he was named Deputy Speaker. During the railway scandal of 1910, he bitterly attacked Premier Rutherford, being one of the leading Liberal "insurgents". Premier Sifton appointed J. R. Boyle, Minister of Education in 1913 and six years later Premier Stewart named him the Attorney General. In the 1921 General election, he ran in two Constituencies: Sturgeon and the multi-member Edmonton riding. He was defeated in the former, but was successful in the latter. He was the Leader of the Liberal Opposition in the

1924. Justice Minister Ernest Lapointe appointed J. R. Boyle a Justice for the Supreme Court Trial Division in 1924.

Boyle died on February 15, 1936 in Ottawa from bronchial pneumonia while on his way to Bermuda.

Source of information:

Canadian Law Lists (1923)

Canadian Parliamentary Guide (1924)

Canadian Parliamentary Guide (1917) p. 459

C. W. W. (1912)

E. Mardon Alberta Judicial Biographical Dictionary (1905-1996) p. 42

Carlson, Debraha 'Debby'

MEMBER OF THE LEGISLATURE 1993-

Born April 5, 1957 in Cereal, Alberta, daughter of Ivan Carlson and Beverly Nagle. She received a Master's degree in administration from Athabasca University and later became an Edmonton accountant. 'Debby' Carlson was returned as the Progressive Conservative Member for Edmonton Ellerslie in 1993. She was re-elected in 1997 and again in 2001.

Source of information:

Canadian Parliamentary Guide, 2002, p. 58

Alberta Who's Who 1994-1998, p. 126

Chadi, Sine

MEMBER OF THE LEGISLATURE 1993-1997

Born February 13, 1956 in Lac La Biche, Alberta, son of Mike Chadi and Zeher Tarrabain. He was an Edmonton businessman. Sine Chadi was returned as the Liberal Member for Edmonton Roper in 1993. He sat as a private member on the opposition side of the Chamber for four years. He did not seek re-election in 1997, but retired from provincial politics at the age of forty-two.

Chambers, Thomas W.

MEMBER OF THE LEGISLATURE 1971-1986

Born July 7, 1928 in Port Arthur, Ontario. Educated at the Port Arthur Collegiate Institute, he attended the University of Toronto, graduating in arts and then receiving an engineering degree. Coming to Alberta, he settled in Edmonton where he became a petroleum-engineering consultant. Interested in Provincial politics, "Tom" Chambers running as a Progressive Conservative, successfully contested Edmonton Calder in 1971. He sat in the Legislature for the next fifteen years. Premier Lougheed appointed Chambers to the Cabinet as Minister of Housing and Public Works in April 1978. He held the Public Works portfolio for eight years. In May 8, 1986 election, he did not seek re-election but retired from politics at the age of fifty-eight.

Source of information:

Canadian Parliamentary Guide (1985)

Canadian Parliamentary Guide (1972) p. 489

Chichak, Catherine

ALDERMAN

MEMBER OF THE LEGISLATURE 1982-1989

Interested in provincial politics, Catherine Chichak, running as a Progressive Conservative, successfully contested Edmonton Norwood in 1971. She sat in the Legislature as a private member on the government side of the house for eleven years. Prior to the 1982 Alberta election, she failed to win her party's nomination. Turning to school board politics, Chichak was elected to the Edmonton Separate school board in the fall of 1983 where she served a term as Board Chairman. In early 1986 Mrs. Chichak won the P.C. nomination for Edmonton Norwood. In the May 8, 1986 general election, she placed second. Later she served as a separate school Trustee and then as an Edmonton Alderman.

Source of information:

Canadian Parliamentary Guide (1985)

Canadian Parliamentary Guide (1972) p. 489

Chivers, Barrie

MEMBER OF THE LEGISLATURE 1990-1993

Born November, 1940 in Ryley, Alberta, son of Oswald Chivers and his wife Enid Slee. He is of English descent and an Anglican. While his primary education was acquired in Ryley, he later pursued undergraduate studies at the University of Alberta, graduating in arts and then in law. Chivers was admitted to the Alberta Bar in 1970 practiced law in Edmonton at the legal firm of Wright and Chivers. In 1971 he was an unsuccessful provincial candidate. However, Barrie Chivers was returned as a New Democrat MLA in the Edmonton Strathcona by-election of December 17, 1990. He sat in the Legislature as an Opposition member for two years. In 1993 he was defeated in his re-election bid by Liberal Al Zaiwny, and retired from politics at the age of 50.

Source of information:

C. L. L. (1995)

Canadian Parliamentary Guide (1992)

Cook, D.B. "Rollie"

MEMBER OF THE LEGISLATURE 1979-1986

Born March 22, 1952 in Edmonton, son oflan M. Cook and Hope McKay Sladon. He attended the University of Alberta and later became an accounts manager for an Edmonton public relations firm. Rollie D. B. Cook was returned as the Progressive Conservative member for the Edmonton Glengarry constituency in 1979. He sat in the Legislature for seven years as a government backbencher. In 1986 he did not seek re-election but retired from politics at the age of thirty-three. In 2003, R. D. Cook was residing in Edmonton.

Source of information:

Canadian Parliamentary Guide (1985)

Canadian Parliamentary Guide (1980) p. 572

Crawford, H. H.

MEMBER OF THE LEGISLATURE 1917-1921

Born March 10, 1878 in Brampton, Ontario, son of Robert Crawford and Melia James. His father was the treasurer for Peel County for many years. After being educated in Brampton, Manitoba, Crawford came to Alberta in 1898, where he became a prominent Strathcona businessman. His titles included merchant, auctioneer, and manufacturer. He served a term as a Strathcona Alderman before the City joined Edmonton. Herbert Howard Crawford served on the Edmonton Public School Board from 1913 to 1917. Interested in Provincial politics, Crawford, running as a Conservative successfully contested Edmonton South in 1913. He entered the Legislature by defeating former Liberal Premier A. C. Rutherford. He sat in the Legislature for eight years as a private member on the opposition side of the House. However, in the 1921 Alberta election, Crawford was defeated at the polls when Edmonton returned all five candidates. Five years later, he again failed to re-enter the Legislature and retired from politics at the age of forty-eight. He was to married Emijoy Kroh of Nebraska, USA, and was a Methodist. Crawford died on January 27, 1945 at the age of sixty-seven.

Source of information: Canadian Parliamentary Guide (1920)

Canadian Parliamentary Guide (1917) p. 460

Crawford, Neil S.

MEMBER OF THE LEGISLATURE 1971-1989

Born May 26, 1931 in Prince Albert, Saskatchewan, son of William F. Craw Cord, originally from Stwicake, Nova Scotia and Hannah Hoen of Canora, Saskatchewan. Educated in Humboldt, he attended the University of Saskatchewan, graduating in Arts. He then received a law degree from the same institution. Coming to Alberta, he settled in Edmonton where he articled under L. Y. Cairns, Q. C. (later Judge Cairns). Crawford was admitted to the bar in 1955. He then joined the Edmonton legal firm of Cormie, Kennedy and Crawford. He was appointed a Q. C. in 1972. While still a University student he became an active member of the Progressive Conservative Party and friend of Alvin Hamilton. After moving to Alberta, he became active in the revitalization of the Conservative Party. From 1961 to 1963, Crawford was the executive assistant to John E. Diefenbaker, then the Prime Minister of Canada. Active in community affairs, he served for

Alderman from 1966 to 1971. Interested in Provincial politics, Neil Crawford successfully contested Edmonton Parkallen in 1971. He was re- elected in 1975, 1979, 1982, and again in 1986 by a marginal victory of 306 votes. Premier Lougheed immediately appointed him to the Cabinet as Minister of Health and Social Development. Four years later he was transferred to the Labor portfolio. In 1979 Crawford was appointed the Attorney General and Government House Leader. He held this position for seven years. In May 1986, Premier Getty appointed Crawford Minister of Municipal Affairs - third in rank in the Cabinet after the Premier and Deputy Premier David Russell. In 1987 he was awared an honorary degree from the University of Alberta. In 1989 Neil S. Crawford did not seek re-election but rather retired from politics. Crawford died on August 24, 1992 in Edmonton after a long illness.

Source of information:

Canadian Parliamentary Guide (1972) p. 490

Decore, Laurence

ALDERMAN 1974-1977

MAYOR 1983-1988

MEMBER OF THE LEGISLATURE 1989-1998

Born June 28, 1940 in Vegreville, son of John N. Decore and Myrosia Decore. His father was the Member of Parliament for Vegreville from 1949 to 1957 and was later a Justice of the Alberta Court of Queens Bench in 1979. Decore was of Ukrainian descent though his surname had been anglicized and Ukrainian Orthodox. Although primarily educated in Vegreville, Decore attended the University of Alberta, graduating in arts and then in law. After being admitted to the Bar, he joined his father's Edmonton law firm. He served as an alderman from 1974 to 1977 and then as the Mayor of Edmonton from 1983 to 1988. Decore was named the Alberta Liberal Leader in October returned as the Liberal Member for Edmonton Glenbarry in 1989. Despite being re-elected in 1994, he resigned his seat in 1999 due to poor health. Decore died shortly afterwards on November 22, 1999.

Source of information:

Canadian Parliamentary Guide (1992)

Diachuk, William Wasyl

ALDERMAN

MEMBER OF THE LEGISLATURE 1971-1986

Born on October 8,1929 in Vegreville, Alberta, son of Nick Diachuk and Helen Drabit. He comes of Ukrainian-Canadian descent. Receiving his primary education in Two Hills, Diachuk then attended the University of Alberta, where he earned a certificate in social work. With his newly acquired education, he then worked as a civil servant for a number of years. Later, Diachuk became a general insurance agent. Active in community affairs, he served on the Edmonton Separate School Board from 1962 to 1971. He was a prominent Ukrainian Catholic. Interested in provincial politics, William Diachuk, running as a Progressive Conservative, successfully contested Edmonton Beverley in 1971. He sat in the Legislature for fifteen years. In 1972 he was named Deputy Speaker of the Legislature. Premier Lougheed appointed Diachuk to the cabinet as Minister responsible for Workers' Health, Safety and Compensation in 1979. Premier Getty reappointed him to the same portfolio in November 1985. In the May 8, 1986 election, Diachuk was defeated in his fourth re-election bid by New Democrat, Ed Ewasiuk and retired from politics at the age of fifty-eight.

Source of information:

Canadian Parliamentary Guide (1985)

Canadian Parliamentary Guide

(1972) p. 490

Duggan, David Milwyn

ALDERMAN

MAYOR

MEMBER OF THE LEGISLATURE 1926-1942

Born May 5, 1879 near Builth, Radnorshire, son of Thomas Duggan and Frances Willia. Educated in Builth, he then pursued an agricultural business career for twelve years. In 1902 he married Marian Price of Preteign, Wales. They had two sons and two daughters. Coming to the District of Alberta, NWT in 1905, he settled in Nanton where he became a successful businessman. In 1912 he moved to Edmonton where he continued his business success and pursued investments. Active in Community affairs, he was elected Mayor of Edmonton in 1921. He held this position for two years. Interested in Provincial politics, David Milwyn Duggan, running as a Conservative, successfully contested the six-member Edmonton Constituency in 1930. He sat in the Legislature for the next twelve years as a private member of the opposition side of the Legislature. He died while still an incumbent in 1942.

Source of information:

Canadian Parliamentary Guide (1942)

Canadian Parliamentary Guide (1934) p. 338

Ewasiuk, Ed

ALDERMAN 1980-1986

MEMBER OF THE LEGISLATURE 1986-1993

Born on September 24, 1933 in Vegreville, son of Nicholas Ewasiuk and his wife Lena. A catholic, he is of Ukrainian descent. Ewasiuk attended the University of Alberta, graduating in education. Following the attainment of his degree, Ewasiuk commenced teaching in Edmonton. From 1974 to 1986 he was the executive director of the Edmonton and District Labor Council. Active in community affairs, Ewasiuk served as Edmonton Alderman from 1980 to 1988. Ed Ewasiuk was returned as a New Democrat Member for the Edmonton Beverly constituency in 1986. He was further re-elected in 1989. A candidate in the June 1993 election, Ewasiuk placed third to Julius E. Yankowsky (the Liberal member for Edmonton Beverly-Belmont).

Source of information: Canadian Parliamentary Guide (1992)

Canadian Parliamentary Guide (1988) p. 693

Ewing, Albert Freeman

MEMBER OF THE LEGISLATURE 1913-1921

Born June 29, 1871 in Elora, Ontario, son of Alexander Ewing, an Irishman, and Mary Manarey, who was of United Empire Loyalist stock. Receiving his primary education in Elora, Ewing then attended the University of Toronto where he graduated with an Arts degree. He then attended the Toronto School of Pedagogy before teaching in Milverton, Ontario. Coming to Alberta in 1899, he settled in Calgary where he studied law under Arthur Sifton, who later became Premier of Alberta. In 1902 he was called to the Northwest Territories Bar. He briefly practiced in Calgary in association with James Short before moving to Edmonton where he became a prominent member of the firm of Ewing and Harvie. A Conservative, he contested Edmonton unsuccessfully in 1909 and again in the 1912 Edmonton by-election. He was returned the Conservative member for Edmonton in 1913 and sat in the Legislature until defeated in 1921. In 1924 he failed in a bid to re-capture an Edmonton seat in the October 27 by-election, being defeated by Liberal W. T. Henry. Justice Minister Hugh Guthrie appointed

Ewing a Justice of the Supreme Court Trial Division in 1931, succeeding Mr. Justice Walsh who was elevated to the Appellate Division. Ten years later he too was elevated to the Appellate Division. Ewing was the first Chairman of the Fanner's Creditor's Arrangement Act Board and held that post until 1935. Mr. Justice Ewing served on the Commission appointed to investigate the Nordegg mine disaster, which cost the lives of more than 100 miners. His report was considered a masterpiece of thoroughness and clarity. In 1904 he married Annie Lafferty of Perth, Ontario, who died in 1933. In 1935 he remarried the former Jean McFarguhar of Thorsby, Alberta. Ewing, a Presbyterian, died on August 28, 1946 in Edmonton. A week before he died, Mr. Justice Ewing had tendered his resignation from the Bench to Justice Minister Louis St. Laurent.

Gariepy, Charles Gerard

MEMBER OF THE LEGISLATURE

Born March 10, 1888 in Montreal, son of Joseph Horindas Gariepy, His brother was Wilfred Gariepy. His father was also the spokesman for the French. He was of ethnic French Canadian descent and a Roman Catholic. His ancestors settled in New France in the 17th century. Coming to the Northwest Territories in 1893, the Gariepy family settled in Edmonton. Educated in Montreal, he later attended both Osgoode Hall Law School and the University of Alberta. During World War One, he enlisted in the Canadian Army and went overseas with the Canadian Expeditionary Force where he saw active service with the 22nd Battalion on the Western Front. In 1919 he was admitted to the Alberta Bar and then became an Edmonton lawyer. An Edmonton lawyer for nine years, he was created a King's Counsel in 1943. Justice Minister Stuart Garson appointed Charles E. Gariepy a judge of the Northern Alberta District Court in 1949. In1963 he retired from the Bench. Gariepy died on September 3, 1976 in Edmonton.

Source of information:

(1917) p. 462

Geldart, S. Gordon

MEMBER OF THE LEGISLATURE 1963-1965

He attended the University of Alberta, graduating in dentistry and practicing in Edmonton. In time, he also became a professor of dentistry at the University of Alberta. Dr. S. Gordon Geldart was returned as the Social Credit member for Strathcona West in 1963 and sat in the Legislature for four years. However, he did not seek re-election, rather opting to return to his academic position at the University. He died in 1980 in Edmonton.

Source of information:

Canadian Parliamentary Guide (1960)

Canadian Parliamentary Guide (1964) p. 471

Gerhart, Edgar Henry

MEMBER OF THE LEGISLATURE 1952-1971

Born on December 18, 1923 in Drumheller, son of Clarence Edgar Gerhart, former Social Credit Cabinet Minister and Mary Celina Chambers, who was of United Empire Loyalist stock from Virginia. Receiving his primary education in Coronation, Gerhart later attended the University of Alberta, graduating in Science and Pharmacy. For ten years he was the pharmacist and proprietor of the Tuck Shop near the University Campus in Edmonton. Interested in Alberta politics, Edgar Gerhart, running as a Social Creditor, successfully contested the multi- member Edmonton Constituency in 1952. With his victory, Gerhart joined his father who had been in the Legislature for twelve years. Notably, this is the only time in Alberta political history that a father and son sat in the Legislature at the same time. In the mid-1950's Gerhart returned to the University to obtain a law degree and was admitted to the Bar in 1960. He sat for a total of nineteen years in the Legislature. In June 1967, Premier Manning appointed Gerhart to the Cabinet as the Minister of Municipal Affairs. In May 1969, Premier Strom appointed Gerhart the Attorney General. He held this position in the Cabinet until he lost his seat in the Legislature in the August 1971 Provincial election. By 1980, Edgar Gerhart was an Alberta Provincial Court Judge.

Source of information:

Canadian Parliamentary Guide (1970)

Canadian Parliamentary Guide (1956) p. 446

Getty, Donald R

MEMBER Of THE LEGISLATURE 1967-1973

PREMIER 1984-1993

Born August 30, 1933 in Montreal, son of Charles R. Getty and Beatrice Hampton. Educated in Toronto, he later attended the University of Western Ontario, graduating in Business Administration. Coming to Alberta, Getty settled in Edmonton where he played as the Quarterback for the Edmonton Eskimos for ten years. He was named "Outstanding Canadian" in the Western Canadian Football League in 1959. He then became an investment counselor and oil consultant. Interested in Provincial politics, Don Getty, running as a Progressive Conservative, successfully contested Strathcona West in 1967. With this victory, Getty sat in the Legislature for the next twelve years. Premier Peter Lougheed appointed Getty the Minister of Federal and Intergovernmental Affairs in 1971. Four years later he was transferred to the Energy and Natural Resources portfolio. In 1979 he did not seek re-election and retired from politics to work in the private sector. However, on October 13,

1985 Don Getty was chosen the Alberta Progressive Leader at an Edmonton Convention and was subsequently sworn in as Premier of Alberta. He entered the Legislature in the December 1985 Edmonton Whitemud by-election and returned for the Edmonton Whitemud Constituency in 1986. After being defeated in Edmonton Whitemud in the 1989 Alberta General election, he re-entered the Legislature by being elected in the May 1989 Stettler by-election. In the March 1992 Progressive Conservative Convention in Calgary, Getty told the delegates that he would lead them into the next Alberta general election. However, he resigned the premiership to Ralph Klein, former Mayor of Calgary in December 1992. In June 1993, Getty did not seek re-election but retired for a second time from politics.

Source of information:

Canadian Parliamentary Guide (1990)

Canadian Parliamentary Guide (1972) p. 493

Gibbs, C. Lionel

MEMBER OF THE LEGISLATURE 1926-1932

Born November 11,1877 in Newport, Monmouthshire, England. Educated in Sutton, Surrey, while from 1886 to 1896 he was at St. John's School, Oxford. He then attended the Newport Technical College, where he studied architecture and drawing. Coming to Alberta in 1907, he settled in Edmonton where he became associated with the architectural firm of Barnes and Gibbs. His firm was the architect for such notable structures as the General Hospital and the Holy Trinity Church. In 1915, Gibbs became an assistant instructor in architecture at the University of Alberta. Early in 1916, he obtained a leave of absence and enlisted in the Canadian Army, serving with the 196th Battalion on the Western Front where he took part in the fighting for Courcellette. At the end of the war, Sgt. Gibbs was appointed to the Khaki University staff at Bramshott, England. On returning to Edmonton, he joined the staff at the Technical School as a mechanical drawing instructor; a position he held until the time of his death. In 1921 Gibbs became an active member in the Labour Movement. He served as the Secretary Treasurer of the Alberta section of the Canadian Labour Party and remained a Labour Alderman for twelve years to the time of his death. Named a Labour candidate, Gibbs successfully contested the multi-member Edmonton Constituency in 1926 and was re-elected in the 1930 General election. In the Legislature, he was regarded as one of the ablest speakers and a strong, cunning debater. A teacher by profession, Gibbs took a great interest in the work of the Alberta Teacher's Alliance, as he was one of the organization's founding members. He believed in education as one of the great forces making for human progress. Gibbs died on September 5, 1932 in Sault Ste. Marie, Ontario. C.

Additional election outcomes in Lionel Gibbs political career include the following: He was an unsuccessful Edmonton Aldermanic candidate in the 1910 election.

Source of information:

Canadian Parliamentary Guide (1931)

Canadian Parliamentary Guide (1934) p. 339

Gibbeault, Gerry

MEMBER OF THE LEGISLATURE 1986-1993

Born March 14, 1953 in Edmonton, son of Norman Gibbeault and Denise Gibbeault. He attended the University of Alberta, graduating in Arts and qualifying as a teacher (a profession he pursued in Edmonton). Gerry Gibbeault, was returned as the New Democrat Member for the Edmonton Millwoods Constituency in 1986 and was re-elected in 1989. However, Gibbeault unsuccessfully ran as a New Democrat Party candidate for the Edmonton Millwoods Constituency in 1983. In 1993, he also failed in his re-election bid as Deborah Carlson, the Liberal Candidate was returned the member for Edmonton Ellerslie. Following his defeat, Gibbeault returned to the classroom.

Source of information:

Canadian Parliamentary Guide (1988) p. 695

Gibbons, Ed

MEMBER OF THE

LEGISLATURE 1997-2001

Born on March 1,1949 in Edmonton, Alberta. Educated in Edmonton, Gibbons attended the Northern Alberta Institute of Technology (NAIT) and became the proprietor of McKinley Heating. Ed Gibbons was returned as the Liberal Member for Edmonton Manning in 1997 where he sat as a private member on the opposition side of the Chamber for four years. In 2001, he was defeated by Tory 'Tony' Vandermeer, in his re-election bid. Gibbons then retired from provincial politics at the age of fifty.

Hancock, D. G.

MEMBER OF THE LEGISLATURE

Born on August 10, 1955 in Fort Resolution, N.W.T., son of Richard Hancock and Kathleen E. Patter. He attended the University of Alberta, graduating in Arts and then in Law in 1979. He was later admitted to the Alberta Bar and became a practicing Edmonton lawyer. David Hancock was returned as the Progressive Conservative member for Edmonton Whitemud in 1997 and was re-elected in 2002. He also served as the Minister of Federal and Intergovernmental Affairs in 1967. He was transferred to the Attorney General department in 1999.

Source of information:

Canadian Parliamentary Guide (2002) p. 612

Hanson, Alice A.

MEMBER OF THE LEGISLATURE 1993

Born May 6, 1927 in Edmonton, Alberta, daughter of Francis Brown and Ruth Trego. She attended the University of Alberta, graduating with an Arts degree. In 1951, she married Oscar Hanson; they have a son and a daughter. She is active in volunteer organizations such as the Boyle Street Co-op. Ms. Hanson was returned as the Liberal Member for Edmonton Highlands in 1993.

Source of information:

Canadian Parliamentary Guide (1996)

Heard, Louis W.

MEMBER OF THE LEGISLATURE 1948-1952 and 1959-1971

Born March 8, 1909 in Crane Lake, Saskatchewan, son of Wesley Heard and Rose Cutting. Educated at Piapot, he then took a banking course from Queen's University. Later he attended the School of Chiropractic at Davenport, Iowa, obtaining a doctoral degree in Chiropractic. Coming to Alberta, he settled in Edmonton where he practiced for the next thirty-five years. Interested in Provincial politics, Dr. "Lou" Heard, running as a Social Creditor, successfully contested the multi-member Edmonton Constituency in 1948, even though he only had 890 votes on the first count. He sat in the Legislature for four years. In 1952 he was dropped from the Social Credit ticket in favor of Dr. J. Donovan Ross. In 1959 Dr. Heard was re-elected as the member for Edmonton North East. This time he sat in election bid by Tory William Diachuk, and retired from politics at the age of sixty-two.

Source of information:

Canadian Parliamentary Guide (1950 and 1970)

Hefferman, Jeremiah

MEMBER OF THE LEGISLATURE 1921-1926

Born January 4, 1884 in Picton, Ontario, son of John J. Hefferman and Ellen Naughton, both of whom had been born in Ireland. Educated in Picton, he later attended Ottawa University and Osgoode Hall Law School, obtaining his Law degree in 1910. He was admitted to the Ontario bar in 1910 and practiced in Toronto for two years.

Coming to Alberta, Hefferman settled in Edmonton. He was admitted to the Alberta Bar in 1913, where he practiced for the next thirty-three years and became a prominent city lawyer. Hefferman was the Prosecuting Attorney for Edmonton for a number of years and was a Crown Prosecutor for Alberta from 1914 to 1919. Notably, in 1921 he was created a King Counsel. An active Roman Catholic, Hefferman was first editor of The Western Catholic (a weekly religious publication) and continued as editor for a number of years. Interested in provincial politics, J. W. Hefferman, running as a Liberal, successfully contested the five-member Edmonton constituency in 1921 in which the Liberals captured all five of the city seats in the election. He sat in the Legislature for five years. Despite this success, in 1926 he failed to win the Liberal nomination and retired from politics. Hefferman continued to practice law in Edmonton until 1945 when he moved to Vancouver. He was admitted to the British Columbia Bar in 1945 and practiced his profession for another 21 years. His name appeared in the Canada Law List in 1969 as still practicing in Vancouver.

Source of information:

Canadian Law List (1969)

Canadian Parliamentary Guide (1925)

Canadian Parliamentary Guide (1926) p. 536

Henry, Michael

MEMBER OF THE LEGISLATURE 1989-1997

Born in 1955, he later became the regional director of the Canadian Mental Health Association. Michael Henry was returned as the Liberal Member for Edmonton Centre in 1989 where he sat in the Legislature for eight years. He was the right hand man for Alberta Liberal Leader Laurence Decore. In 1997 Michael Henry won the Liberal nomination for the Edmonton West riding at the Liberal association nominating convention. However, Prime Minister Chretien declared that law professor A. Anne McLennan was the official liberal candidate.

Source of information:

Canadian Parliamentary Guide (1994)

Henry, William Thomas

ALDERMAN

MEMBER OF THE LEGISLATURE 1924-1926

Born January 2, 1872 in Prince Edward Island. Came to the District of Alberta, NWT in 1890, and settled in Calgary where he was in the dry goods business. Three years later he moved to Edmonton where he became a prominent businessman. Notably, Henry was the proprietor of Blowey-Henry retail furniture firm for forty years. Active in community affairs, Henry served as the Mayor of Edmonton for three years. He also served on the hospital board. Interested in Provincial politics, William T. Henry, running as a Liberal, unsuccessfully contested Edmonton West in 1917. He placed second, losing to Conservative A. F. Ewing. Seven years later Henry, running again as a Liberal, successfully contested the October 27, 1924 Edmonton City-Wide by-election; He was a candidate under the proportional representation system of voting. This was the first election in count, Henry was ahead of A. F. Ewing by 402 votes, while Henry M. Bartholomew, the Communist with labor endorsement placed third. Henry was eventually elected on the second count. Interestingly, this is the only election in Alberta history that a Communist candidate received more than thirty percent of the vote. Henry sat in the legislature for two years. In 1926 he failed in his re-election bid and died on March 12, 1952 in Hollywood, California. He was recognized as one of Edmonton's oldest pioneer businessmen.

W. T. Henry's political life is further highlighted in his tenure as a successful Edmonton Aldermanic candidate in the 1901 and 1902 elections. He also served as the Mayor of Edmonton from 1914 to 1918.

Source of information:

Canadian Parliamentary Guide (1925)

Hewes, Betty

MEMBER OF THE LEGISLATURE 1986-1993

Born March 12, 1924 in Brampton, Ontario, she later attended the University of Toronto. In 1949 she married F. William Hewes, with whom she has four children. From 1964 to 1967 she was the executive Director of the Canadian Mental Health Association. Active in community affairs, Mrs. Hewes served as an Edmonton Alderman from 1974 to 1984. In 1984 she was appointed the chairman of the Board of Canadian National. Betty Hewes was returned as the Liberal Member for Edmonton elected in 1989 and again in 1993. On the retirement of Laurence Decore, she became the acting Alberta Liberal Leader until November 12, 1994 when Grant Mitchell was returned as the Liberal Leader after a questionable phone-in voting system.

Source of information:

Canadian Parliamentary Guide (1966)

Canadian Parliamentary Guide (1988) p. 697

Hiebert, Alois Patrick

MEMBER OF THE LEGISLATURE 1982-1986

Born June 4, 1938 in Humboldt, son of Bernard Hiebert and his wife Anne. Educated at Muenster's St. Peter's College. He also attended the University of Saskatchewan, the University of Alberta, and the University of Oregon. At the University of Alberta, he pursued a degree in education and then became an Edmonton Teacher. In time he became the principal of St. Joseph High School. Alois P. Hiebert was returned as the Progressive Conservative member for the Edmonton Gold Bar constituency in 1979 where he sat in the Legislature for the next six years. He was eventually defeated by Liberal Betty Hewes in 1986. In 1990 he was still an Edmonton School principal. He is a Roman Catholic. In 1960 he married Lorraine Thilodeau of Edmonton; they have four children.

Source of information:

Canadian Parliamentary Guide (1980) p. 575

Hohol, Albert Edward 'Bert'

MEMBER OF THE LEGISLATURE 1971-1979

Born on December 27,1922 in Two Hills, Alberta, son of George H. Hohol and of Ukrainian descent. During World War II, Hohol enlisted in the Royal Air Force and saw active service in Europe. Receiving his primary education in Two Hills, he later attended the University of Alberta, graduating in Education in 1950. From 1947 to 1967, he taught in the Edmonton district. Later, he received his Master's of Education from Alberta 1954 and his doctorate from the University of Oregon in 1967. By 1970 Hohol was the Associate Superintendent of the Edmonton Public Schools. Interested in Provincial politics, Dr. Bert Hohol, running as a Progressive Conservative, successfully contested Edmonton Belmont in 1971 and sat in the legislature for 8 years. Premier Lougheed appointed Dr. Bert Hohol Minister of Manpower and Labor (1971-1975). In 1979 he did not seek re-election and opted to retire from politics.

Source of information:

Canadian Parliamentary Guide (1972) p. 495

Holowach, Ambrose

MEMBER OF THE LEGISLATURE 1959-1971

Born July 22, 1914 in Edmonton, Alberta, son of Sam Holowach and Josephine Dwornik. He was of ethnic Ukrainian descent and a Ukrainian Catholic. Educated in Edmonton, he then went to Europe where he was a music journalist at the Salisbury festival from 1931 to 1936. His writing career was also accompanied by his experience as an accomplished musician. Holowach later returned to Edmonton where he became a successful businessman; he was the proprietor of a dry cleaning company. Interested in federal politics, Ambrose Holowach, running as a Social Creditor, unsuccessfully contested the Edmonton East riding in the 1949 general election. Four years later, he was elected in the 1953 general election and was re-elected in the 1957 general election. He sat in parliament for five years on the opposition benches. In 1958, he was defeated by Tony William Skoreyko. Turning to provincial politics, Holowach successfully contested Edmonton Centre in 1959 and sat in the Legislature for the next twelve years. Premier Manning took him into cabinet October 15, 1962 as the Provincial Secretary and Premier Strom re-appointed him to this portfolio in December 1968. However, in 1971 Holowach was defeated by Peter Lougheed's former executive assistant, David King, by 100 votes in his re-election bid in the Edmonton Kingsway Constituency. Holowach then retired from politics at the age of fifty-seven. He was a bachelor.

Source of information:

Canadian Parliamentary Guide (1935)

Canadian Parliamentary Guide (1970)

Canadian Parliamentary Guide (1960) p. 461

Horan, John W.

MEMBER OF THE LEGISLATURE 1963-1971

Born May 13, 1908 in Sheffield, England, son of John W. Horan and Ann Roberts, both of whom were of Irish ancestry. Educated in Sheffield, he then attended night school where he studied mining, mathematics, and science for 4 years. He was a Baptist. In the 1920's Horan worked in the Sheffield Coal Mines. He came to Canada in 1929 or 1930, going as a mining prospector to Ontario, Saskatchewan and the Territories for ten years. He finally came to Alberta in 1940, where he was employed as a clerk at Edmonton's Woodwards department store. Later, Horan was a proprietor of his own hardware store in Jasper Place for twenty years. Active in the Social Credit League, John W. Horan won the party's nomination for Edmonton Jasper Place in 1963 by defeating the incumbent member Herbert Jamieson. In the June 17, 1963 General election, he was elected with a 1405 vote majority over his nearest rival, Liberal Keith C. Campbell. Horan sat in the Legislature as a private member on the government benches for eight years. In 1971 he was not a candidate for re-election as he decided to retire from politics at the age of sixty-three. In 1987 he was residing in Edmonton.

Source of information:

Canadian Parliamentary Guide (1970)

Canadian Parliamentary Guide (1964) p. 474

Howard, Super*

Information not retrieved

Howson, William Robinson

MEMBER OF THE LEGISLATURE 1930-1935

Born March 6, 1883 in Norwood, Ontario, son of William R. Howson and Ann Johnston. He was also educated in his hometown of Norwood. Howson's first job was teaching in an ungraded school near Peterborough. He then became a bank clerk; in a profession in which he greatly excelled. By 1906, he was the youngest bank manager in Canada, working for the Sovereign Bank in Stirling, Ontario. He came to Alberta in 1910, where he became a Calgary real estate agent. In 1911, he campaigned for Sheriff G. Van Wart, the Liberal candidate for the Federal riding of Calgary. Howson later attended the University of Alberta, graduating in Arts with a gold medal in 1915, and in Law the next year. He articled with A. G. MacKay and was called to the Alberta Bar in 1915. He was admitted to the Alberta Bar that same year. Howson then enlisted in the Canadian Army, serving as a Sergeant with the tank corps in France for two years. After the war, he entered the firm of Parlee, Freeman, and Howson. A life-long Liberal, he won a seat in the multi-member Edmonton Constituency in 1930. Two years later, he was named the Alberta Liberal Leader. He won re-election in 1935, but resigned his seat the next year. Justice Minister Ernest Lapointe appointed Howson a Justice of the Supreme Court, Trial Division in 1936. He transferred to the Appellate Division in 1942. In 1944, he was named Chief Justice of the Supreme Court, Trial Division. During World War II, Howson presided at a German prisoner-of-war murder trial in Medicine Hat. William R. Howson died on June 25, 1952, while still on the Bench. He was sixty-nine years of age. It should be noted that in the early 1930's, many thought that W. R. Howson would be the Premier of Alberta after the next general election. However, the UFA government toppled in 1935, not by the Liberals, but by the Social Credit Movement led by William Aberhart.

Source of information:

Canadian Law List (1934)

Canadian Parliamentary Guide (1934) p. 341

Hutton, Drew

MEMBER OF THE LEGISLATURE **2001-**

Drew Hutton was returned as the Progressive Conservative Member for Edmonton Glenora in 2001. He is sitting as a private member on the government side of the Chamber.

Source of information:

Canadian Parliamentary Guide (2002) p. 614

Hyndman, Louis David 'Lou'

MEMBER OF THE LEGISLATURE 1967 - 1993

Born July 1, 1935 in Edmonton, son of Louis Davies Hyndman Sr., K. C. and Muriel MacKintosh. He is of English descent and an Anglican. His great-great-grandfather Benjamin Davies served as the Colonial Secretary of Prince Edward Island prior to Canadian Confederation in 1867. His great-grandfather Sir Louis Henry Davies (born 1845) sat in the P. E. I. Legislature from 1872 to 1879 serving as Premier from 1876 to 1879. He vacated his seat to enter federal politics and was returned as the Conservative member for the Queen's riding (P. E. I.) in 1891. Hyndman served in the federal cabinet from 1896 to 1901 when he was appointed a Justice of the Supreme Court of Canada. His great-grandson 'Lou' Hyndman was educated in Edmonton where he attended the University of Alberta, graduating in Arts and a further degree in Law. He was admitted to the Alberta Bar in 1960 and practiced law with his father's legal firm of Field, Hyndman, Field. 'Lou' Hyndman was returned as the Progressive Conservative member for Edmonton West in 1967. He was the executive assistant to the Minister of Citizenship and Immigration from 1962 to 1963. He became the Minister of Federal and Intergovernmental Affairs and Government House Leader in 1975. Four years later he became the Provincial Treasurer, holding this portfolio for seven years. In 1986 he did not seek re-election and retired from politics at the age of 50. Years later he served as Chancellor of the University of Alberta in the 1990s. By 2002, he was retired.

Source of information:

Canadian Law List (1996)

Canadian Parliamentary Guide (1990)

Canadian Who's Who (2002)

Canadian Parliamentary Guide (1968) p. 481

James, Norman B.

MEMBER OF THE LEGISLATURE FOR ACADIA (1935-1940) AND FOR EDMONTON (1940-1948)

Born in 1872 near London, England. James came to Alberta as

a young man in 1891 and was a cowboy near Calgary. Eight years later, he settled on a farm near Lethbridge. From there he moved to Winnipeg, where he was an accountant. Later James settled permanently in Youngstown, where he became a prominent farmer. He became well known across East Central Alberta as a Minister of the Gospel who gave his service, without pay. One of the original members of the Social Credit movement, James successfully contested Acadia in 1935, defeating the sitting UFA member, Lorne Proudfoot. He sat one term in the Legislature for Acadia, before successfully running in the multi-member Edmonton Constituency in 1940. James retired from politics in 1948, after 13 years in the Legislature. His column in the Social Credit publication "Today and Tomorrow" was popular for many years. N. B. James died December 13, 1961 in Edmonton.

Source of information:

Canadian Parliamentary Guide (1946)

Canadian Parliamentary Guide (1945) p. 374

Jamieson, Frederick Charles

MEMBER OF THE LEGISLATURE 1931-1935

Born May 18, 1875 in Carleton County, Ontario, son of James Jamieson and Mary Ann Craig. He was of English-Ulster-Scottish descent and an Anglican. Educated at Kemptville, he then qualified as a teacher and taught in rural Ontario for two years. In 1895 he came to the Northwest Territories where he homesteaded near Lacombe. He later moved to Strathcona and became a law articling student with A. C. Rutherford. Jamieson was admitted to the Northwest Territories Bar in 1899 and practiced law in the firm of Rutherford Jamieson. Jamieson volunteered for military service and saw action with the Canadian Mounted Rifles in the South African War. After the war he returned to Strathcona continuing as a prominent Edmonton lawyer for the next 70 years. During World War I he

Canadian Expeditionary Force where he saw active service as the Commander of the First Canadian Division Mounted Troopers. After the war he again returned to his Edmonton legal practice. Colonel F. C. Jamieson was returned as a Conservative member for Edmonton in the 1931 by-election. He sat in the Legislature for five years in opposition. In 1935 he was defeated in his re-election bid and retired from politics at the age of 60. He died on October 4, 1966.

Source of information:

Canadian Law List (1955)

Canadian Parliamentary Guide (1934)

Canadian Parliamentary Guide (1934) p. 341

King, David Thomas

MEMBER OF THE LEGISLATURE 1971-1986

Born June 22,1946 in Perth, Ontario, son of Rev. Albert Edward King and Ethel Dickson. Educated in Lethbridge and Edmonton, he attended both Victoria University and the University of Alberta. In 1967, while still a student, he became the executive assistant to the leader of the opposition, E. Peter Lougheed. David T. King was returned as the P.C. member for Edmonton Highlands in 1971. He was 25 years of age. Premier Lougheed appointed King to the Cabinet in 1979 as the Minister of Education. In 1986 he was defeated in his re-election bid by New Democrat Pamela Barrett. He then retired from politics at the age of forty. King is now a prominent Edmonton businessman.

Source of information:

Canadian Parliamentary Guide (1972) p. 497

Lakaszuk, Thomas

MEMBER OF THE LEGISLATURE 2001-

Born April 5, 1969 in Poland. He attended the University of Alberta graduating in education and became an Edmonton Teacher. He also served as a translator and interpreter for the Crown's Prosecutor's office. Thomas Lukaszuk was returned as the Progressive Conservative member for Edmonton-Castle Down riding in 2001.

Source of information:

Canadian Parliamentary Guide (2002) p. 620

Laing, Marie (nee Sprado)

Born July 30,1937 in Stettler, Alberta, daughter of William Sprado and his wife Jean Burtch. She attended the University of Alberta- Calgary campus where she received her teaching certificate. She then became a schoolteacher in Stettler in 1958. Later Laing returned to the University of Alberta Edmonton campus, graduating in Arts (1973) and later with a Masters degree (1979). A Unitarian and psychologist, Ms. Laing was the Director of the Edmonton sexual assault center from 1978 to 1982. Marie Laing was returned as the New Democrat Member for the Edmonton Avonmore constituency in 1986 and was re-elected in 1989. In 1993, she failed in her re-election bid and retired from politics. Liberal Eugene Zwozdesky, a teacher, was returned as the Member for Edmonton Avonmore.

Source of information:

Canadian Parliamentary Guide (1988) p. 702

Leibovici, Karen

MEMBER OF THE LEGISLATURE

Born May 27, 1952 in Montreal, Quebec, daughter of Poldi Leibovici and Gertrude Schafer. She attended McGill University, graduating with a bachelor and then a Master's degree in Social Work. With her new education, she became industrial relations consultant. Karen Leibovici was returned as the Liberal Member for Edmonton Meadowlark in 1993 and sat as an opposition member for eight years. In the 2001 general election she was defeated by Tory Robert Markell. She then retired from politics at the age of forty-nine.

Source of information:

Canadian Parliamentary Guide (1998-1999) p. 588

LeMessurier, Mary

MEMBER OF THE LEGISLATURE 1979-1986

Born June 12, 1929 in Montreal, Quebec, she is of ethnic French descent. LeMessurier attended McGill University and then qualified as a nurse at the Royal Victoria Hospital. She married Ernest Power and they have four children together. Mary J. LeMessurier was returned as the Progressive Conservative member for Edmonton Centre in 1979. Premier Lougheed appointed Ms. LeMessurier the Minister of Culture in March 1979. In 1986 she was defeated by NDP member Rev. William Roberts. Later she served as the Alberta Trade Commissioner in London.

Source of information:

Canadian Parliamentary Guide (1985)

Canadian Parliamentary Guide (1980) p. 580

Lakaszuk, Thomas

Born April 5, 1969 in Poland, Lakaszuk came to Canada as a child. He attended the University of Alberta, graduating with an education degree with which he became a teacher. Thomas Lakaszuk was returned the Progressive Conservative Member for Edmonton Castle Downs in 2001.

Lymburn, John Farquhar

MEMBER OF THE LEGISLATURE 1935-1940

Born September 20, 1880 in Ayr, Scotland, son of William Lymburn and Margaret Farquhar. Educated at Ayr Academy, he also attended Glasgow University and became a qualified lawyer. Migrating to Alberta, he settled in Edmonton and was admitted to the Alberta Bar in 1911. He became a prominent Edmonton lawyer for the next fifty-five years and was created a King's Counsellor. John Farquhar Lymburn was returned as a United Farmer of Alberta member for the Multi-Edmonton constituency in 1926. Notably, he lead the vote on the first count and sat in the Legislature for nine years. Premier Brownlee immediately appointed Lymbum the Attorney General; a position he held for nine years. In 1935 he ranked fifth for the six-member Edmonton Constituency but was edged in later counts under the transferable voting system. Lymburn then retired from politics at the age of fifty-five. In the September 22, 1942 Edmonton by-election Lymburn, running as an Independent, failed in his bid to re-enter the Legislature. He continued to practice law in Edmonton into the late 1960's. In 1937, J. F. Lymburn's name was mentioned in the Social Credit scandalous "Banker's Toadies" pamphlet that resulted in the Social Credit member for Edson (John Unwin) being sent to prison for in sighting "murder."

Source of information:

Canadian Law List (1937, 1938)

J. Blue "Alberta. Past and Present" (1924) v. 3, p. 269

Canadian Parliamentary Guide (1939)

A. P. P. (1924)

A. McRae "The History of Alberta," (1924)

Canadian Parliamentary Guide (1934) p. 342

Koziak, Julian Gregory J.

MEMBER OF THE LEGISLATURE 1971-1986

Born September 16, 1940 in Edmonton, son of John Koziak and Marie Waytkiw. He attended the University of Alberta , graduating in Arts (1962) and in law (1963). Koziak was admitted to the Alberta Bar in 1964 and then joined the Edmonton legal firm of Kosowan and Wachowich. Interested in provincial politics, Julian Koziak, running as a Progressive Conservative, successfully contested Edmonton Strathcona in 1971 and sat in the Legislature for the next fifteen years. Premier Lougheed appointed him to the cabinet as Minister of Education in 1975. Four years later he was transferred to consumer and corporate affairs. In 1982 he was named Minister of Municipal Affairs and in November 1985 the new premier, Don Getty, confirmed the appointment. In the May 8, 1986 election Koziak was defeated at the polls. When Premier Lougheed retired, Koziak was one of the three candidates who sought to replace him as the Progressive Conservative Alberta leader. In the October 1985 leadership convention he placed second, losing to Don Getty. Koziak later pursued a life as a businessman.

Source of information:

Canadian Law List (1970)

Canadian Parliamentarv Guide

(1985)

Canadian Parliamentary Guide (1972) p. 497

Knaak, Peter

MEMBER OF THE LEGISLATURE 1979-1982

Born October 28, 1942 in Hamburg, Germany. Coming to Alberta as a child, Knaak attended the University of Alberta, graduating in Arts and then in Law. He was admitted to the Alberta Bar in 1972 and then became a prominent Edmonton lawyer. Peter Knaak was returned as the Progressive Conservative member for the Edmonton Whitemud constituency in 1979. He sat in the Legislature for three years as a government back bencher. In 1982 he did not seek re-election but retired from politics at the age of forty. In 1990 Knaak was created a Queen's Counselor and in 1991 he became a member of the Edmonton legal firm of Cleal, Pahl and Knaak.

Source of information:

Canadian Law List (1986)

Canadian Parliamentary Guide (1981)

Canadian Parliamentary Guide (1980) p. 5778

MacAdam, Lt. Roberta Catherine (Nurse)

Born June 21, 1881 in Sarnia, Ontario, daughter of Robert MacAdam, a newspaper publisher, and his wife Catherine Brown. She was an Anglican of Anglo-Irish descent on her paternal side. Although her primary education came from Guelph, she later attended Chicago University. As a young woman, MacAdam came to Alberta and settled in Edmonton where she was in charge of the Domestic Science department of the government. She also helped in the establishment of women's institutes across rural Alberta. At the outbreak of World War I, Miss MacAdam enlisted in the nursing corps. She received a commission and went overseas with the Canadian Expeditionary Force and served in the United Kingdom. In the Special Overseas Soldier legislative election to send two service personnel to the Legislature, Lt. MacAdam and Padre Captain (Methodist) Robert Pearson were returned. Initially she sat as Miss MacAdam, but on September 21, 1920 she married her brother's law partner, Harvey Stinson Price, of Calgary. In 1921 she did not seek re-election and retired from provincial politics. The Prices homesteaded for a decade in the Peace River Country before finally settling in Calgary. Notably, MacAdam was one of the five Alberta women who in 1929 persuaded the British Privy Council that women were persons under the law and could be summoned to sit in the Canadian Senate. Lieutenant Catherine Roberts was the first Edmonton woman to sit in the Legislature.

Source of information:

Canadian Parliamentary Guide (1934)

MacBeth, Nancy [See Nancy Betkowski / MacBeth]

McClelland, Ian

Born June 22, 1942 in Trail, B. C., son of Al McClelland and Edith Steardin. He attended Edmonton's, Northern Alberta Institute of Technology and became a photographer. Ian G. McClelland was returned the Liberal Member for Edmonton Southwest in 1993. Later, Ian McClelland was returned again as the Liberal Member for Edmonton Rutherford riding in 2001.

McClung, Mrs. Nellie (Nee Mooney)

Born October 20, 1873 in Chatsworth, Ontario, daughter of John Mooney and his wife Letitia McClung. She was of Scotch-Irish descent. McClung's family moved to Manitoba when she was seven, but she did not go to school until she was ten. But by the time she was sixteen, she had her teaching certificate and was teaching in the Sourie Valley. In 1896 she married Robert Wesley McClung and they had four children together. Nellie McClung became a short story writer and prominent in the Manitoba suffragette movement. She was also active in the Women's Christian Temperance Union. Arriving in Alberta in 1915, she persuaded premier Sifton to introduce legislation giving women the right to vote. The legislation was passed on April 15, 1916 . Nellie McClung was returned as the Liberal Member for the Multi-Edmonton Constituency in 1921 and she sat in the Legislature for five years as a vocal opposition member. In 1926, she did not seek re-election and retired from politics at the age of fifty-three. In 1933 she moved to Vancouver. Mrs. McClung was associated with the group of "The Famous Five" women who established the fact that in Canada "Women" were also persons and as such could be appointed to the Senate. Others in this group included Louise McKinney (former Member of the Alberta Legislature, from the Claresholm, constituency (She was the first women to be elected)), Emily Murphy of Edmonton, Henrietta Edwards of Fort MacLeod, and Irene Parlby, Member of Legislative Assembly for Ponoka. McClung was a Methodist and an active Prohibitionist. She died on September 1, 1951 in Victoria.

Source of information:

Canadian Parliamentary Guide (1925)

Canadian Parliamentary Guide (1926) p. 539

Macdonald, Hugh F.

MEMBER OF THE LEGISLATURE 2001-

Born August 5, 1955 in Souris, P.E. I., son of Donald F. Macdonald and Anne Howlett. He had a career in oilfield construction. Hugh F. Macdonald was returned as the Liberal member for Edmonton Gold Bar in 1997 and was re-elected in 2001. He is sitting as a private member on the opposition side of the Chamber.

Source of information:

Canadian Parliamentary Guide (2002) p. 621

Macdonald, Hugh John (Edmonton)

MEMBER OF THE LEGISLATURE 1940-1944

Born November 11, 1898 in South Hanson, Mass., USA, son of Daniel MacDonald and Nellie O'Brien. Hugh MacDonald attended the University of Alberta, graduating in Arts and then in Law in 1923. He was admitted to the Alberta Bar in 1925 and was a well- known Edmonton lawyer for the next nineteen years. Active in community affairs, he served as an Edmonton Alderman from 1934 to 1940. Interested in provincial politics, Hugh John MacDonald successfully contested the five-member Edmonton constituency as an Independent in 1940. He sat in the Legislature for four years and then was appointed a judge in the Trail Division of the Supreme Court in 1944. Thirteen years later he was elevated to a Justice in the Appellate Division.

Source of information:

Canadian Parliamentary Guide (1945) p. 375

Canadian Law List (1944)

McDougall, John Alexander

MEMBER OF THE LEGISLATURE 1909-1913

Born on May 20, 1854 in Oakville, Victoria County, Upper Canada, son of Alexander J. McDougall and Janet Cummings. Both of his parents had been born in Scotland. McDougall was educated at Woodville. In 1879 he settled permanently in Edmonton where he became a millionaire merchant in the McDougall Second firm. Active in civic affairs, McDougall was returned as the Mayor of Edmonton in 1907. He signed the papers for the construction of the High Level Bridge across the North Saskatchewan River. John A. McDougall was returned as a Liberal member for the two-member Edmonton constituency in 1909. During the 1910 railway scandal debate, he spoke and voted against the Liberal Rutherford administration. McDougall sat in the Legislature for four years. In 1913 he did not seek re-election and retired from politics at the age of fifty-nine. He was a Presbyterian. McDougall died on December 17, 1928 in Edmonton.

Source of information:

Canadian Parliamentary Guide (1912) p. 524

MacEachern, Alex D.

MEMBER OF THE LEGISLATURE 1986-1993

Born September 27, 1939 in Hinton Trail in the Peace River Country of Northern Alberta, son of Ian S. MacEachem and Isabella E. J. Karr. He is of Scotch descent. MacEachern attended the University of Alberta, graduating in Education in 1965 and in Arts in 1975. Applying his education, MacEachern became a schoolteacher for twenty-four years. Politically, he served as the treasurer of the Alberta New Democratic Party from 1976 to 1983. After being defeated in the 1979 and 1982 elections, Alex MacEachern was returned the New Democratic member for the Edmonton Kingsway constituency in 1986. He was then re-elected in 1989. However, in 1993 he failed, as did all of the New Democratic Members - a total of eighteen - to win re-election. Lance White, an Edmonton Alderman from 1983 to 1992, was returned as the Liberal

Mayfield.

Source of information:

Canadian Parliamentary Guide (1986-1993)

Canadian Parliamentary Guide (1988) p. 704

McInnis, John

MEMBER OF THE LEGISLATURE 1989 -1993

John McInnis was the New Democrat member from 1989 – 1993.

Mack, William

MEMBER OF THE LEGISLATURE 1979-1982

In the late 1970's, Mack was the business manager of the Amalgamated Transit Union and a director of the local Authorities Pension Board. William Mack was returned as the Progressive Conservative member for the Edmonton Belmont constituency in 1979 and sat in the Legislature for three years as a government backbencher. In 1982 he did not seek re-election. Rather, he retired from politics at the age of fifty-eight. In 1991 he was living in retirement in Edmonton.

Source of information:

Canadian Parliamentary Guide (1981)

Canadian Parliamentary Guide (1980) p. 582

McKinnon, Randolph Hugh

MEMBER OF THE LEGISLATURE (1959-1967)

Born July 22, 1917 in Delburne, Alberta, son of John Donald McKinnon and Ruth Rebecca. He was of Scotch/Swedish descent. Initially educated in Delburne, he then attended the Calgary Normal School where he qualified as a teacher. He later received an Education degree from the University of Alberta and pursued a career as an Edmonton schoolteacher. In 1943 McKinnon married Margaret Maureen Marshall, daughter of James A. Marshall, Social Credit, MP for Camrose from 1935 to 1949. They had three daughters. R. H. "Randy" McKinnon was returned the Social Credit member for the Strathcona West constituency in 1959 where he sat in the Legislature for the next eight years. In 1964, Premier Manning appointed McKinnon to the cabinet as the Minister of Education. While minister, McKinnon gave a University Charter to the Calgary campus of the University of Alberta in 1966 and created the University of Lethbridge in 1967. In 1967 McKinnon was defeated in his second re-election bid by Progressive Conservative Donald R. Getty. McKinnon later served as the superintendent of the Northland school division. He is an Anglican. In 1991 R. H.McKinnon was living in retirement in Edmonton.

Source of information:

Canadian Parliamentary Guide (1966)

MacClelland, Ian

McLennan, Andrew R.

ALDERMAN

MEMBER OF THE LEGISLATURE 1923-1926

Born 1871 in Walkerton, Ontario, son of Thomas McLennan and Barbara Little. He was of Scotch descent. McLennan became a wealthy Kenora lumber merchant. Coming to Alberta in 1912, he settled in Edmonton where he operated a lumber yard. In 1903 he married Annette L. Pray, daughter of his long time business partner. They had a son and two daughters. A.R. McLennan served as an Edmonton Alderman from 1919 to 1921. He then was returned as a Liberal member for the multi-member Edmonton constituency. In 1925 he resigned his seat in the Legislature in order to enter federal politics. However, he failed to win a seat in the House of Commons. A. R. McLennan died on April 9, 1943.

Source of information:

Canadian Parliamentary Guide (1925)

Main, Douglas C.

MEMBER OF THE LEGISLATURE 1989-1993

Born July 18, 1946 in Willow Bunch, Saskatchewan, son of Claude Bruce Main and his wife Lillian Marie Belleflour. Douglas Cameron Main was educated at St. Boniface and Winnipeg's Winston Churchill High School. He also attended the University of Athabasca, graduating in Administration in 1967. Main commenced his broadcasting career with CJOB Radio Station in Winnipeg in 1970. Also in 1970 he married Judith, daughter of Joshua Summer. They have two sons. Coming to Alberta in 1975, Douglas Main settled in Edmonton where he became a well-known personality with CITV. He unsuccessfully ran as the Reform Party candidate for the Edmonton Strathcona Federal Riding in 1988. Douglas Main was returned as the Progressive Conservative member for the Edmonton

Parkallen Constituency in 1989. Premier Getty appointed Douglas Main to the Cabinet as the Minister of Culture and Multiculturalism. In 1992 he was an unsuccessful provincial conservative candidate when Ralph Klein won the leadership. He was not a candidate in the 1993 election.

Source of information:

Canadian Parliamentary Guide (1992)

Manning, Ernest Charles (Premier)

MEMBER OF THE LEGISLATURE 1935-1968

EDMONTON SENATOR 1970-1983

Born September 20, 1908 in Carnduff, Saskatchewan son of George Henry Manning and his wife Elizabeth Mara Dickson. He is of English descent. Receiving his primary education in Rosetown, Manning later attended the Calgary Prophet Bible Institute. After completing his studies, he remained at the Institute as it's secretary and was an assistant to William Aberhart. He was closely associated with Aberhart's fundamental Christianity and later advocated the economic theories of Major Douglas' Social Credit while helping to organize the Alberta Social Credit movement. Ernest Manning at the age of twenty-seven was returned as the Social Credit member for the multi-member Calgary constituency in 1935. He sat in the Legislature for thirty-three and a half years, first representing Calgary and after 1940, representing Edmonton. Premier Aberhart appointed Manning to his cabinet as Provincial Secretary and Minister of Trade and Industry in 1935. On Aberhart's death, in 1943, the Social Credit Caucus named Ernest Manning its Leader, and thus premier of Alberta in 1943. He held this position for twenty-five years. In 1952 he became his own Minister of Mines and Minerals and then also his own Attorney General in 1955. He served as the Provincial Treasurer from 1944 to 1954. Manning was recognized as an able bureaucrat and clever politician. This is exemplified as he led his Social Credit League to a series of seven Alberta General election victories between 1944 and 1969. He was a small 'c' conservative. After the discovery of oil in the Leduc oil field in 1947, he managed the resulting two decades of prosperity. Alberta changed from a 'have not' province to a 'have' under his stewardship. Manning's administration was remarkable for it's lack of corruption; despite huge budgetary surpluses, government growth was controlled. His three ablest Cabinet ministers were Nathan Elder Tanner, member for Cardston from 1935 to 1952, who encouraged foreign petroleum companies to search for petroleum in the province; Gordon Taylor, member for Drumheller from 1935 to 1979, who as Minister of Highways improved ease of travel; and Andre Olaf Halborg, member for Alexandra from 1948 to 1971, who as the Minister of Education in the 1950's and 1960's supervised the growth of schools and the Universities in Alberta. Premier Manning had a quiet and retiring manner and was recognized by friend and foe as an honest politician. The rapid growth of the Reform Party may be due in part because of the 'northism' of the "Manning Era." In 1967 he was made a Privy Counselor. In January 9, 1969, Manning resigned his seat in the Legislature and retired from the premiership. He later became a director for the Imperial Bank of Commerce. Prime Minister Trudeau appointed Manning to the Senate on October 7, 1970; a position Manning held for thirteen years. On September 23, 1983, he retired from politics. In 1991 Manning moved from Edmonton back to Calgary.

Manning was a prominent Baptist preacher all his life. In 1936 he married Muriel, the daughter of William Preston of Calgary, and they had two sons. One son, E. Preston Manning is the National leader of the Reform Party of Canada. In 1992 Ernest Manning and Lucien Maynard were the only serving members of the Legislature to be first elected in 1935. He was residing in Calgary.

Source of information:

Canadian Parliamentary Guide (1936)

Canadian Parliamentary Guide (1945) p. 376

Canadian Parliamentary Guide (1967)

Canadian Parliamentary Guide (1980)

Canadian Who's Who, 1980

Martin, Ray

MEMBER OF THE LEGISLATURE 1982-1993

Born August 4, 1941 in Drumheller, Alberta, son of James Martin and Olive Kathryn Churchill. Initially educated in Delia, Alberta, he then attended the University of Alberta, graduating with an Education degree. Martin became a Calgary schoolteacher, while attending the University of Calgary where he received a Masters of Science degree. In 1977 he married Cheryl Matheson and they had five children. In 1975 Ray Martin unsuccessfully contested, running as a New Democratic candidate, the Calgary McKnight constituency. Later he moved to Edmonton. Ray Martin was returned as the New Democratic Member for Edmonton Norwood in 1982. He was re-elected in 1986 and again in 1989. On the death of Grant Notley, Ray Martin was named the Alberta Leader of the New Democratic Party on November 12, 1984. In the 1993 Alberta general election, Ray Martin and all the other New Democrats in the Legislature were defeated. In 1994 Martin resigned the party's leadership and became an insurance agent.

Source of information:

Canadian Parliamentary Guide (1992)

Canadian Parliamentary Guide (1985) p. 695

Markell, R. Bob

MEMBER OF THE

LEGISLATURE 2001-

Markell attended the University of Alberta, graduating in Education. He became a teacher and served as the principal of Jasper Place Composite High School. Robert 'Bob' Markell was returned as the Progressive Conservative Member for Edmonton Meadowlark in 2001. He is sitting as a private member on the government side of the Chamber

Source of information:

Canadian Parliamentary Guide (2002) p. 622

Mason, Brian

MEMBER OF THE LEGISLATURE 2000 (By-election)

After attending the University of Alberta, Mason became a bus driver. He served eleven years as an Edmonton Ward 3 Alderman. Brian Mason was returned as the New Democratic Party member in the Edmonton Highlands June 12,2000 by-election and was re-elected in the 2001 general election.

Source of information:

Canadian Parliamentary Guide (2002)

Massey, Donald

MEMBER OF LEGISLATURE 1993-

Born 1936 in Edmonton, son of Frederick James Massey, Jr. and Helen Josephine Bishop. Educated in Edmonton, he attended the University of Alberta, graduating in Education. He then attended the University of Kansas, graduating with a Master's in education and later a doctoral degree. Dr. Donald was an Education professor at the University of Alberta, when he became active in provincial politics. Donald Massey was returned as the Liberal Member for Edmonton Millwoods and was re-elected in 1997 and again in 2001. He was a front bench critic of the ruling Progressive Conservative government.

Source of information:

Canadian Parliamentary Guide (2002)

Masky, Gary

MEMBER OF THE LEGISLATURE 2001-

Born in High Prairie in northern Alberta. He became the proprietor of an oilfield servicing firm. Gary Masky was returned as the Progressive Conservative Member for Edmonton Norwood in 2001.

Source of information:

Canadian Parliamentary Guide (2002)

Miller, Abe W.

ALDERMAN

MEMBER OF THE LEGISLATURE 1955-1959

Born March 25, 1897 in Budapest, Hungary, son of Oseas Muhlstock Miller and Gertrude Tilleman. He came to Canada in 1899 as a child and was educated in Dufferin, Manitoba and Montreal, Quebec. As a young man, Miller came to Alberta and settled in Edmonton where he attended Alberta College. He later entered the University of Alberta and obtained a law degree in 1925. Miller was admitted to the Alberta Bar the same year. Miller became a prominent Hebrew Edmonton lawyer and businessman and practiced in the city for the next forty years. In 1941 he was awarded a K.C. Active in civic affairs, he served for years as a city Alderman in the 1950's, was a Royal Alexandra Hospital Board member, and was a director of the Edmonton Exhibition Association. Miller was also a prominent member of the Liberal Party. Interested in provincial politics, Abe Miller successfully contested the multi-member Edmonton constituency in 1955. Notably, he was the first Jew to be elected to the Alberta Legislature. He sat in the Legislature on the front bench of the opposition for four years. In 1959 he was defeated in his bid to retain his Legislative seat. (His son, Tevie Miller, practiced law in his father's law firm in the 1950's and 1960's, before he was appointed a federal Alberta judge.) He also served as the Chancellor of the University of Alberta in the 1980's.

Source of information:

Canadian Law List (1966)

Canadian Parliamentary Guide (1958)

Canadian Parliamentary Guide (1959)

Miniely, Gordon Thomas W.

MEMBER OF THE LEGISLATURE 1971-1979

Born October 25, 1939 in Bonnyville, son of Gordon Miniely and his wife Irene Hazel. He was an Anglican. Gordon T. W. Miniely was returned as the Progressive Conservative member for Edmonton Centre in 1971 and sat in the Legislature for eight years. Premier Lougheed appointed him Provincial Treasurer in his first cabinet. In 1975 Miniely was transferred to the Hospitals and Medical Care portfolio. He retired from politics in 1979. In 1998 he was the senior partner in the Miniely and Towers firm of chartered accountants in Edmonton.

Source of information:

Canadian Parliamentary Guide (1978)

Canadian Parliamentary Guide (1972) p. 499

Mitchell, Grant

MEMBER OF THE LEGISLATURE 1986-1997

Born July 19, 1951 in Ottawa, son of Donald W. Mitchell. He was a Roman Catholic. Mitchell attended the University of Alberta, graduating in Arts, and Queen's University obtaining a Masters. He became a civil servant before he became the Vice President of the Edmonton Principal Group from 19979 to 1986. Mitchell was returned as the Liberal member for Edmonton Meadowlark in 1986 and sat in the Legislature for twelve years (the last as the Alberta Liberal Leader). He resigned his seat in 1998 so that Nancy MacBeth, his replacement as the Liberal leader, could enter the Legislature.

Source of information:

Canadian Parliamentary Guide (1995) p. 572

Mjolsness, Christine

MEMBER OF THE LEGISLATURE 1986-1993

Born June 29, 1955 at Coronation, Alberta, Christine Mjolsness's father was of Ukrainian descent and her mother, who served as a Town Councilor, was of Norwegian descent. The surname is Scottish. Christine Mjolsness (pronounced Melsness) attended the University of Alberta graduating in Education in 1978. She then taught in elementary schools in Donalda and Jasper before moving to Edmonton and Lorelei School. She was a teacher for the Public System until she was given leave to work with Catalyst Theatre on a child sexual assault prevention program. Interested in Provincial politics, Christine Mjolsness, running as a New Democrat, unsuccessfully contested Edmonton Calder in 1982. She placed third with 32% of the vote. Turning to Federal politics, she unsuccessfully contested the Wetaskiwin riding in the September 1984 General election, placing second, losing to Conservative incumbent Stan Schellenberger (only receiving 13% of the vote). However, in the May 8, 1986 Alberta general election, Christine Mjolsness was elected as the New Democrat Member for the Edmonton Calder constituency. She had a 2210 vote majority over her closest opponent, Conservative Tony Falcone. In the Legislature, Mjolsness was the New Democrat Social Services critic. In 1993, she failed in her re-election bid.

Source of information:

Canadian Parliamentary Guide (1992)

Canadian Parliamentary Guide (1988) p. 706

Morrish, Walter

MEMBER OF THE LEGISLATURE 1936-1937

Born October 19, 1890 in the County of Devon, England, son of Henry Morrish and Julia Morrish. His father was a master carpenter. On leaving school, Morrish was apprenticed to the drapery business in Shrewsbury and stayed there two years. Coming to Alberta in 1909, young Morrish, who planned to become a missionary, delivered letters to Rev. Dr. George Kerby in Calgary. He worked in Calgary for a year before enrolling at Edmonton's Alberta College. Morrish took his matriculation into the University of Alberta, where he took an active part in urging the formation of a medical school. Later he was a member of the first medical class and then transferred to McGill University, Montreal, from which he graduated in Medicine in 1918. While working his way through medical school, during the summer he would work with a construction crew building the Grand Truck Pacific rail line west of Edmonton. Dr. Morrish then became a house surgeon at Montreal's Royal Victoria Hospital. During the final months of World War I, he enlisted in the Canadian Army, serving as a medical officer on troop transports crossing the u-boat infested waters of the North Atlantic. After the war, Dr. Morrish served as a Methodist medical missionary in Northern Alberta and was stationed at the Smokey Lake hospital for four years. He then did a year's post-graduate medical studies in Cambridge and London, England. On his return to Canada, Dr. Morrish established a medical practice in Edmonton where he became a prominent physician. Interested in education, he served on the Edmonton public school board for six years. A Liberal, Dr. Walter Morrish unsuccessfully contested the six-member Edmonton constituency in 1935. In a field of twenty-seven candidates, he placed eighth. In June 1936, he was elected at the by-election caused by the death of Liberal, G. H. Van Allen. On being appointed to the federal civil service in 1937, Dr. Morrish resigned his seat in the Legislature. Dr. Walter Morrish died on January 30, 1974 at the age of eighty-four.

Source of information:

Canadian Parliamentary Guide (1937)

Mullen, David B.

MEMBER OF THE LEGISLATURE 1935-1940

Born November 7, 1885 in Peterborough, Ontario, son of Richard Mullen and his wife Isabella Mahood. He was of English-Irish descent. Arriving in Alberta as a young man, Mullen became an Edmonton district farmer and livestock dealer. David Bertrum Mullen was returned as a Social Credit member for the multi-member Edmonton Constituency in 1935 and sat in the Legislature for five years. Premier Aberhart appointed Mullen to his cabinet in 1937 as the Minister of Agriculture. Previously the Premier had fired the former Minister W. W. Chant. In 1940 Mullen was re-elected as the Social Credit member for the Camrose Constituency in order that Ernest Manning could be elected in Edmonton. David B. Mullen died while still a sitting member in October 1940. He was a Presbyterian prominent Freemason and former member of the Ku Klux Klan.

Source of information:

Canadian Parliamentary Guide (1938)

Canadian Parliamentary Guide (1936) p. 390

Norris, Mark

MEMBER OF LEGISLATURE 2001-

Born in Edmonton, son of Paul J. Norris, a former Alderman, and Doree (Micky) Cohn. Educated in Edmonton, he attended St. Francis Xavier University, Antigonish, Nova Scotia, graduating in Arts and became a small Edmonton businessman.

Mark Norris was returned as the Progressive Conservative Member for Edmonton McClung in 2001 by defeating Liberal Nancy MacBeth (Betkowski). Premier Ralph Klein immediately took him into the cabinet as the Minister of Economic Development.

Source of information:

Canadian Parliamentary Guide (2002)

O'Conner, Charles Gerald

ALDERMAN

MEMBER OF THE LEGISLATURE 1935-1940

Born December 3, 1890 in Walkerton, Ontario, son of Frederick Sheppard O'Connor and Maria Isabella Hamilton. He was an Anglican of Anglo-Irish descent. O'Conner's elder brother, George Bligh O'Connor (q.v.), became Chief Justice of Alberta. Educated in Edmonton, O'Conner attended Alberta College. He then studied law at York's Osgoode Hall and read law with Griesbach and O'Connor in 1912 and 1913. He was admitted to the Alberta Bar in 1914. During World War I O'Conner enlisted in the army and went overseas as an officer with the Canadian Expeditionary Force. He was in active service with the machine gun corps on the Western Front. After the war he returned to Edmonton where he joined the prominent legal firm of Griesbach, O'Connor and O'Connor. Active in civic politics, he served as an Alderman in 1932 and 1933. He was also a president of the Edmonton Chamber of Commerce. C. Gerald O'Connor was returned as the Liberal member for the multi-member Edmonton constituency in 1935 and sat in the Legislature as an opposition member. In 1940 he was narrowly defeated at the polls and retired from politics to return to his prior legal profession. He had been created a King's Counsel in 1939 and in 1945 was appointed a Judge of the Federal Exchequer Court. O'Conner died on November 16, 1949 in Ottawa.

Source of information:

C. L. L. (1939)

Canadian Parliamentary Guide (1939)

Canadian Parliamentary Guide (1936) p. 390

Olson, Susan

MEMBER OF THE LEGISLATURE

Page, J. Percy

MEMBER OF THE LEGISLATURE 1940-1948 and 1952-1959

LIEUTENANT GOVERNOR 1959-1964

Born May 14, 1887 in Rochester, New York, son of Ian Bell Page and Elizabeth Teresa Thomas. Both of his parents were Canadian by birth. Coming to Canada in 1890, Page was educated at Milton Collegiate Institute before he attended Ontario Normal School where he qualified as a teacher. He later attended Queen's University where he graduated in Arts in 1913. Venturing to Alberta, he settled in Edmonton where he taught at the Commercial High School and later became the principal. Page also organized and coached the "Edmonton Grads" women's basketball team in 1914. Under his tutelage, the Grads won the world title for 17 consecutive years. J. Percy Page was returned as an Independent Member for the multi-member Edmonton Constituency in 1940. He sat in the Legislature from 1940 to 1948 and again from 1952 to 1959 as a Conservative member. In 1959, he was defeated by Social Creditor Richard H. Jamieson in the Jasper West Constituency. Page then proceeded to retire from politics at the age of seventy-two. Prime Minister Diefenbaker appointed J. Percy

Page Lieutenant Governor of Alberta on December 19, 1959. In 1961 he was awarded an honorary doctoral degree from the University of Alberta. He held the post of Lieutenant Governor for five years.

Source of information:

Canadian Parliamentary Guide (1947)

Canadian Parliamentary Guide (1958)

Canadian Parliamentary Guide (1962)

Canadian Parliamentary Guide (1945) p. 378

Canadian Parliamentary Guide (1960) p. 446

Pahl, Milton G.

MEMBER OF THE LEGISLATURE 1979-1986

Born October 30, 1943 in Hanna, Alberta, son of Packy E. Pahl and Rose Hardinges. Educated in Hanna, he then attended the University of Alberta, first graduating in Arts and then studying for a Masters in Business Administration. Pahl used his education to become an Edmonton management consultant. Milton George Pahl was returned as the Progressive Conservative member for the Edmonton Mill Woods constituency in 1979. He sat in the Legislature for seven years. Premier Lougheed appointed Pahl a minister without portfolio responsible for Native Affairs in 1982. In 1986 Pahl was defeated by New Democrat Gerry Gibeault. He then retired from politics at the age of forty-three. In 1991 Milton Pahl was the proprietor of Native Venture Capital Company in Edmonton.

Source of information:

Canadian Parliamentary Guide (1985)

Canadian Parliamentary Guide

(1980) p. 5

Pannu, Raj

MEMBER OF THE LEGISLATURE 1997-

Attended the University of Alberta and was a rural schoolteacher before moving to Edmonton where he was again a teacher. Later Panu became a professor at the University of Alberta. Raj Pannu was returned as the New Democratic Party member for Edmonton Strathcona in 1997 and was re-elected in 2001. He is one of the two N. D. P. members of the 83-member Legislature. He was named his party's leader in February 2000.

Paproski, Carl

MEMBER OF THE LEGISLATURE 1982-1986

Born January 25, 1945 in Edmonton, son of Alexander Paproski and his wife Anna Pastuchuk who was of ethnic Ukrainian descent. He is a Roman Catholic. The family had resided at Lowow before coming to Canada in 1930. Paproski also had two elder brothers: Steven E. Paproski and Dr. Kenneth R. H. Paproski had been active in politics. Steve had sat in the House of Commons for 25 years while Kenneth sat in the Legislature for eleven years (1971-1982). Educated in Edmonton, Carl had attended the University of Alberta, graduating in Sciences and qualifying as a teacher. He later received a Masters of Education degree and became a teacher with the Edmonton Separate School Board. Carl M. Paproski was returned as the P. C. member for Edmonton Kingsway (Dr. Paproski's old constituency) in 1982. He sat in the Legislature for four years as a private member on the government side of the Chamber. In 1986 he did not seek re-election and retired from politics at the age of forty-one.

Source of information:

Canadian Parliamentary Guide (1985) p. 701

Paproski, Kenneth Henry

MEMBER OF THE LEGISLATURE 1971-1982

Born January 17, 1931 in Edmonton, son of Alexander Paproski, a Pole, and his Ukrainian wife Anne Pastuschuk. The family had migrated to Canada from Poland. He is of ethnic Ukrainian descent on his maternal side. His elder brother was Steve E. Paproski, an M. P. for 25 years and his young brother Carl M. Paproski, an M.L.A. Educated in Edmonton, Kenneth also attended the University of Alberta, graduating in Sciences and then in Medicine in 1956. He became an Edmonton physician. In 1955 he married Louise Elsie, daughter of Howard Cherniak of Edmonton. They have three children together. Dr. Robert R. H. Paproski was returned as the P. C. member for Edmonton Kingsway in 1971. He sat in the Legislature for eleven years as a private member on the government side of the Chamber. In 1982 he did not seek re-election but retired from politics. In the Canadian Medical Directory (1999) Dr. Paproski is listed as an Edmonton physician.

Source of information:

Canadian Parliamentary Guide (1985)

A. M. D. (1988)

Canadian Parliamentary Guide (1972) p. 499

Paul, Pamela

Prevey, Warren W.

MEMBER OF THE LEGISLATURE 1926 - 1930

ALDERMAN

Born September 23, 1874 in Elroy, Wisconsin, son of Francis Prevey and Mary Bissett. Both of his parents had been born in central Canada. Educated in Elroy, Prevey attended the University of Wisconsin in Madison. Coming to the District of Alberta, N.W.T., he settled in Edmonton where he became the manager of City Dairy, and a Director of Alberta Salt Company and the Arctic Ice Firm. He served as an Alderman from 1918 - 1919 and as a Liberal member of the Legislature from 1926 to 1930. However, he did not seek re-election and retired from politics at the age of fifty-six.

Source of Information:

Canadian Parliamentary Guide (1929)

Prowse,J. llarper

MEMBER OF THE LEGISLATURE 1945-1959

SENATOR 1966-1976

Born on July 2, 1913 in Taber, Alberta, son of James H. Prowse Sr., a Taber lawyer, and his wife Elizabeth Short Colquhoun. He was of ethnic Scottish descent and an Anglican. Educated in Mifford, he the attended the Edmonton Normal School. Prowse later attended the University of Alberta and graduated in Arts, pursuing a careers as an Edmonton newspaper reporter. During World War II he enlisted in the Canadian Army and saw active service in the Italian campaign in 1944. Unfortunately, he was seriously wounded. In January 1945 he was elected to represent the army in the Alberta legislature and sat in the Chamber for 14 years. In 1947 Prowse was chosen as the Alberta Liberal leader; a position he held for 11 years. While a member, he attended the University of Alberta and graduated with a degree in Law. He was admitted to the Alberta Bar in 1958. In 1959 he did not seek re-election. He was an unsuccessful federal candidate in 1962 and 1963. Prowse was summoned to the Senate in 1966 where he sat for ten years. He died in 1976.

Source of information:

Canadian Law List (1960)

Canadian Parliamentary Guide (1947)

Canadian Parliamentary Guide (1958)

Canadian Parliamentary Guide (1975)

Canadian Parliamentary Guide (1950) p. 435

Ruddstaach, G. Joseph

Ramsey, James

ALDERMAN

MEMBER OF THE LEGISLATURE 1917-1921

Born April 14, 1864 in Imlay City, Michigan, son of John Ramsey and Agnes Davidson. He came to Canada when he was four with his parents and was educated in Oxford County, Ontario. At the age of 13, he started working in a Platsville general store where he remained for seven years. Subsequently, he was engaged in business in Toronto,

Montreal, New York and Guelph. Arriving in Alberta in 1911, Ramsey established the firm of James Ramsey in Edmonton and for the next 20 years he was one of the city's most prominent businessmen. In 1929 he sold his business to the T. Eaton Company. He was for several years a director of the Canadian National Railway. Ramsey served a term as an Edmonton Alderman prior to entering provincial politics in 1917. A Conservative, he successfully contested Edmonton East and sat in the assembly until 1921. However, he did not seek re-election. Ramsey was also the president of the Northern Alberta Conservative Association for a number of years. In addition to these accolades, he was the honorary Colonel of the Edmonton regiment. He was a Methodist. Died December 23, 1937 in his winter home at Cable Beach, Nassau, Bahaman Islands.

Source of information:

Canadian Parliamentary Guide (1920)

Canadian Parliamentary Guide (1917) p. 468

Rathgeber, Brent, M

Born July 24, 1964 in Melville Saskatchewan. He attended the University of Saskatchewan, initially graduating with a degree Public Administration and then in Law (1990). He is now an Edmonton lawyer. He was admitted to the Alberta Bar in 1991 and gazetteed a Queen's Counsel in 2001. Brent Rathgeber was returned as the Progressive Conservative Member for the Edmonton Calder Constituency in 2001.

Source of information:

Canadian Parliamentary Guide (2002) p. 629

Roberts, Rev. William A.

MEMBER OF THE LEGISLATURE 1986-1993

Born July 22, 1954 in Hamilton, Ontario, son of Edward W. Roberts and his wife Elsie Irene Leslie. He is of English descent and an Anglican. Roberts attended Trent University, graduating in Arts in 1976, and then Harvard University Divinity School (M. Div., 1979) and was ordained an Anglican priest. Later he was a Rockefeller Scholar at Princeton University. Roberts came to Alberta where he became the vicar at All Saints Anglican Cathedral. William Roberts was returned as the New Democratic party member for Edmonton Centre in 1986 and he sat in the Legislature for seven years acting as Federal and Intergovernmental Affairs critic. In 1993 he did not seek re-election and retired from politics at the age of forty-eight.

Source of information:

Alberta Business Who's Who Directory (1992) p. 329

Canadian Parliamentary Guide (1988) p. 713

Roper, Elmer Ernest ***** (delete?)

MEMBER OF THE LEGISLATURE 1943-1949 and 1952-1955

Born June 4, 1893 in Igonish, Nova Scotia, son of Franklin Roper and Annette MacDonald. Roper was educated in Sydney. Coming to Alberta as a young man, he settled in Edmonton and later became the publisher of The People Weekly Bulletin Mineworker. Active in community affairs, Roper served as an Edmonton Public School Trustee from 1925 to 1929. Roper was unsuccessful in running for a seat in the Legislature in 1926,1930 and 1940 and for the House of Commons in 1935. E. Roper was returned as the C. C. F. member for the Edmonton Constituency in the September 22, by election. He sat in the Legislature for something years while serving as the Alberta C. C. F. something Something E. Roper served as an Edmonton Alderman something was elected Mayor of Edmonton in 1959. He held this position for four years. He did not seek re-election in 1963. something married Golhe Bell. They had four children, including Lyall something Roper celebrated his 70th Wedding anniversary in 1984. In 1993 he was living in retirement in Edmonton.

Source of information:

Canadian Parliamentary Guide (1945) p. 379

Ross, Dr. J. Donavan

MEMBER OF THE LEGISLATURE 1952 - 1971

Born March 13, 1911 in Waldo, B.C., son of Joseph W. Ross and Violet Brown. He was of Scottish descent and a member of the United Church. Initially educated in British Columbia, Ross later attended the University of Alberta, graduating in Arts and then in Medicine. During WWII he served as the Medical Officer of the H.M.C.S. Sturgeon and saw active service in the North Atlantic. After the war he became an Edmonton physician. Dr. J. Donovan Ross was returned as the Social Credit member to the Legislature as an Edmonton Member of the Multi-Member Constituency in 1952. He served for 19 years. Premier Manning appointed Ross to the Cabinet in 1957 as the Minister of Health. In 1959 he was returned as the Social Credit Member for Strathcona Centre. He held the Health portfolio from 1957 to 1969 when Premier Strom transferred him to Natural Resources. He was defeated in 1971 by Tory Julian Koziak. He then retired from provincial politics.

Source of Information:

Canadian Parliamentary Guide (1956) p. 455

Canadian Parliamentary Guide (1971)

Rutherford, Alexander C.

Sapers, Howard

MEMBER OF THE LEGISLATURE 1993-2001

Born November 24, 1957 in Toronto, son of Edward Sapers and Phyllis Caplan. He attended Simon Fraser University, graduating in Criminology. Sapers became the executive director of the John Howard Society of Alberta. Howard Sapers was returned as the Liberal Member for Edmonton Glenora in 1993 where he sat as a private member on the opposition side of the Chamber for eight years. In 2001, he was defeated in his re-election bid by Progressive Conservative candidate Drew Hutton. Sapers then retired from provincial politics at the age of forty-four.

Source of Information:

Canadian Parliamentary Guide (1994) p. 544

Schmid, Horst A

MEMBER OF THE LEGISLATURE 1971-1986

Born April 29, 1933 in Munich, Bavaria, Germany, son of Karl L. Schmid. Coming to Canada as a young man in 1952, Schmid studied Grade XII education after his arrival. By the early 1970's he was an Edmonton businessman connected with the export trade. Interested in provincial politics, Horst Schmid running as a Progressive Conservative, successfully contested Edmonton Avonmore in 1971. He sat in the legislature for fifteen years. Premier Lougheed appointed Horst Schmid Minister of Culture, Youth, and Recreation in 1971. Notably, he held the culture portfolio for eight years. From 1979 to 1982 Schmid was Minister of State for Economic Development/International Trade and from 1981 to 1986 he was Minister of International Trade. In 1986 he placed second, losing to Marie Laing of the NDP by a mere 93-vote margin. Schmid, after retiring from politics, was named the Commissioner General for Alberta Trade and Tourism in 1986.

Source of information:

Canadian Parliamentary Guide (1972) p. 500

Sekulic, Peter

MEMBER OF THE LEGISLATURE 1993-1997

Born in 1962, he was of Ukrainian descent. Sekulic attended the University of Alberta, graduating in Arts and becoming an Edmonton social worker. Peter Sekulic was returned as the Liberal Member for Edmonton Manning in 1993. He sat as a private member on the opposition side of the Chamber for four years. In 1997 he did not seek re-election and retired from provincial politics at the age of thirty-five.

Source of information:

Canadian Parliamentary Guide (1995) p. 576

Sloan Linda

Linda Sloan was a Liberal member of the Legislature from 1993 - 1997

Szwender, Walter

MEMBER OF THE LEGISLATURE 1982-1986

Born October 20,1950 in Edmonton, son of Walter Szwender Sr. and his wife Wanda Godawa. He was of ethnic Ukrainian descent and a Catholic. Szwender attended the University of Alberta graduating in Education; he later became an Edmonton teacher. Walter R. Szwender was returned as the PC member for Edmonton Belmont in 1982. He sat in the Legislature for four years as a private member on the government side of the chamber. In 1986 he was defeated by the New Democrat candidate Thomas Sigurdson. In 1989 Szwender was again defeated at the polls.

Source of information:

Canadian Parliamentary Guide (1985)

Canadian Parliamentary Guide (1985) p. 714

Taft, Kevin

Kevin Taft was returned as the Liberal member for Edmonton Riverside in 2001.

Tanner, Howard E.

MEMBER OF THE LEGISLATURE 1955 - 1959

Born December 4, 189[illegible] in

Tilsonburgh, Ontario, son of Harry Tanner and Elizabeth Kissick. He was of English descent and a Protestant. Educated in Stratford, he later attended Queen's University, graduating in Arts in 1926 and the University of Alberta, graduating with a Master's Degree in 1932. During WWI Tanner enlisted in the Canadian Army and saw active service with the 49th Battalion on the Western Front. By 1930 he was an Edmonton teacher. He was the principal of the University High School for years. During his political career, Tanner also served as an Alderman. Howard E Tanner was returned as a Liberal Edmonton member in 1955. He sat as an opposition member for four years. In 1959 he did not seek re-election but rather opted to retire from politics. Later, he moved to Toronto.

Source of information:

Canadian Parliamentary Guide (1956) p. 457

Canadian Parliamentary Guide (1959)

Tomyn, William

MEMBER OF THE LEGISLATURE 1935-1952 and 1959-1971

Born in September of 1905 in Warwick, Alberta, son of Maxim Tomyn and his wife Nancy Boychuk, He was of ethnic Ukrainian descent and a Catholic. Receiving his primary education in Vegreville and Edmonton, he Tomyn later attended the Calgary Normal School, qualifying as a teacher. He pursued this profession in Willingdon. William Tomyn was returned as the Social Credit member for Whitford in 1935. He sat in the Legislature for a total of thirty years from 1935 to 1952 and again as the Social Credit member for Edmonton Norwood from 1959 to 1971. In 1971 he did not seek re-election and retired from politics at the age of sixty-five. Interestingly Tomyn and Alfred J. Hooke, a member for Rocky Mountain House, were the last two of the class of '35 to vacate their seats.

Source of information:

Canadian Parliamentary Guide (1950)

Canadian Parliamentary Guide (1970)

Canadian Parliamentary Guide (1936) p. 392

Canadian Parliamentary Guide (1960) p. 469

Van Allen, George Harold

MEMBER OF THE LEGISLATURE 1935-1937

Born on June 22, 1890 in Morrisburg, Dundas County, Ontario, son of W. A. Van Allen. Van Allen was educated at Morrisburg Collegiate Institute. Coming to Alberta as a young man in 1910, he attended the Calgary Normal School, qualifying as a teacher. Van Allen taught in Lethbridge for two years before enrolling at the University of Alberta, where he took Law. He was admitted to the Alberta Bar in 1915 and established a law firm in Edmonton. He was created a King's Counsel in 1930. A Liberal, G. H. Van Allen successfully contested the multi-member Edmonton constituency in 1935. He sat in the Legislature until the time of his death. During the campaign, Van Allen maintained that Alberta, like the Maritimes, had been bled to death by the tariff structures for years and that the agreement at Confederation had been broken by the federal government. He died on June 15, 1937 in Edmonton at the young age of forty-six.

Source of information:

Canadian Parliamentary Guide (1936-1937)

Canadian Parliamentary Guide (1936) p. 393

Canadian Who's Who, 1936

Vandermeer, A. 'Tony'

Born on October 8, 1962 in Edmonton. He attended NAIT and later became the proprietor of Integra Homes. Tony Vandermeer was returned as the Progressive Conservative member for Edmonton Manning in 2001.

Source of Information:

Canadian Who's Who (2002) p. 634

Weaver, D. S. D. Charles Yardley

ALDERMAN

MEMBER OF THE LEGISLATURE 1926-1930

Born June 9, 1884 in Liverpool, England, son of Thomas Charles Weaver and his wife Laura. He was of English descent and an Anglican. Weaver received his primary education at Manchester Grammar School. In 1903 he came to Western Canada as a Barr Colonist and homesteaded near Mannville. Later he attended the University of Alberta and graduated in law. He was admitted to the Alberta Bar in 1915. Previously Weaver had enlisted in the First Edmonton Fusiliers in 1909. He became a sergeant two years later. He was commissioned a lieutenant in the Alberta Dragoons and two years later promoted to captain. Weaver went to Europe as an officer with the 49th Battalion. It is highly probable that he saw more front line active service then any other officer in the unit. For his efforts, Weaver was awarded the Distinguished Service Order for Bravery. By the autumn of 1918 he was second-in-command of the 49th Battalion in the last campaign of the war. After the war Weaver became a prominent Edmonton lawyer. Active in civic politics, he served as an Alderman from 1922 to 1923. Colonel Charles Y. Weaver was returned as a Conservative member of the multi-member Edmonton constituency in 1926. He was re-elected in 1930, but died on October 1, 1930 at the age of forty-six.

Source of information:

Canadian Law List (1929)

Canadian Parliamentary Guide (1929)

White, Lance

MEMBER OF THE LEGISLATURE 1986-1989 and 1993-1997

Born August 31, 1946 in Winnipeg, Manitoba. Coming to Alberta as a young man, he settled in Edmonton where he attended the University of Alberta, graduating in Civil Engineering in 1971. He then became an Edmonton engineer and later a consulting engineer. Lancelot D. White was elected an Edmonton Alderman in 1983. He was re-elected in 1986 and again in 1989. However, in 1989 he failed in his bid to be elected as the Liberal member for the Provincial Edmonton Calder constituency. However, four years later, Lancelot D. White was returned as the Liberal Member for the Edmonton Manning constituency in the June 1993 general election.

Source of information:

Canadian Parliamentary Guide (1996)

Wickman, Percy

MEMBER OF THE LEGISLATURE 1989-1997

Born June 10, 1941 in Port Arthur, Ontario. Coming to Alberta as a young man, he settled in Edmonton where he later attended the Northern Alberta Institute of Technology (NAIT) and the University of Alberta, graduating in Political Science in 1973. From 1973 to 1976 he was the executive director of the Handicapped Housing Society of Alberta and was also a part-time instructor at Grant MacEwan College. Percy D. Wickman served as an Edmonton Alderman from 1977 to 1986. Three years later, he was returned as the Liberal Member for the provincial Edmonton Whitemud constituency in 1989. Wickman defeated Premier Don Getty and was re-elected the member for Edmonton Rutherford in 1993. However, he did not seek re-election in 1997 and retired from politics.

Williams, F. William

MEMBER OF THE LEGISLATURE 1944-1948

Born in England in the 1890's. At the outbreak of World War I, he enlisted in the British Army, serving with the Welsh regiment on the Western Front. Later he transferred to the Royal Flying Corps and served in Egypt. After the war, Williams came to Alberta and settled in Edmonton. For many years, he was employed by the Alberta Liquor Board. At the outbreak of World War II, he enlisted in the Canadian Army, serving with the Edmonton Loyals in Europe for two years. In 1943, he was sent back to Canada receiving an honorable discharge. He then became the secretary/treasurer of the Edmonton branch of the Canadian League. Interested in politics, Williams successfully contested the five member Edmonton constituency in 1944 as a Veteran candidate and sat one term in the Legislature. He was not a candidate in the 1948 general election. Williams died on April 4, 1969 in Edmonton.

Source of information:

Canadian Parliamentary Guide (1947)

Canadian Parliamentary Guide (1945) p. 410

Wilson, Ethel Sylvia

Born February 13, 1902 in Sunnyside, Alberta, son of Frank Knight and Elizabeth Spooner. Her father was an unsuccessful candidate for the provincial Sturgeon constituency in 1905. She attended the Edmonton Business College. Miss Knight married David Wilson in 1925. They farmed in the Namao district, north of Edmonton. Active in civic affairs, Mrs. Ethel Wilson served as an Edmonton Alderman from 1952 to 1966. Mrs. Wilson also was the Social Credit member for the provincial Edmonton North constituency from 1959 to 1971. She was taken into the Manning cabinet in 1962 as a minister without a portfolio. In 1968 she was re-appointed by Premier Strom and held this position until 1971. She was a Pentecostal.

Source of information:

Canadian Parliamentary Guide (1960) p. 470

Woloshyn, Stan

MEMBER OF THE LEGISLATURE 1989-

He is of ethnic Ukrainian descent. His ancestor Dmytro Woloszin married Katarzyna Balasz in 1901 at Beaver Lake, Alberta. Woloshyn became a school teacher and was the principal of Kitaskinaw school, Enoch Indian reserve, west of Morinville from 1977 to 1989. Stanley Woloshyn was returned as the New Democratic Party member for Stony Plain in 1989. He was re-elected as the Progressive Conservative Member in 1993 and again in 1997. In 1996 premier Ralph Klein appointed him to the cabinet as the Minister of Public Works, Supply, and Services. Later Woloshyn was transferred to the Community Development portfolio. In 2002, he was the minister of Senior's Concerns.

Source of information:

Canadian Parliamentary Guide (2002)

Woo, Henry

MEMBER OF THE LEGISLATURE 1979-1989

Born March 18,1929 in Lethbridge, son of Ming Woo and his wife Ida Woo. He was of Chinese descent and an Anglican. Educated in Edmonton, Woo attended military courses at both naval and air force schools, and from 1950 to 1955 he served in the Royal Canadian Air Force. Politically, Woo served on the federal cabinet sub-committee on Indian Economic Development and was Executive Assistant to the federal Minister for Northern Development and Indian-Metis Liaison. He was also Executive Assistant to the provincial Minister of Recreation, Parks and Wildlife. Henry Woo was returned as the Progressive Conservative member for Sherwood Park in 1979 and he sat in the Legislature for 10 years. In 1989 he did not seek re-election, rather retiring from politics at the age of 60. He returned to a private career as a management consultant with a special interest in trade and development. Notably, Woo was awarded the Order of Canada in 1987.

Source of information:

Canadian Parliamentary Guide (1980) p. 594

Wright, Gordon S. D.

Born June 28, 1927 in Kingston, Jamaica, son of Alwyn Dales Wright and his wife, Mavis Parsons. He was of English descent and an Anglican. Wright was an unsuccessful candidate for the New Democratic Party in 1967, 1975, 1979 and 1982. However, Gordon S. D. Wright was returned as the New Democratic member for Edmonton Strathcona in 1986 and he sat in the Legislature for four years. He died on October 18, 1990 while still an incumbent.

Yankowsky, Julius

MEMBER OF THE LEGISLATURE 1993-

Born August 8, 1938 in Lamont, Alberta, son of Walter Yankowsky and Helen Olinyk. He is of ethnic Ukrainian descent. Educated in Lamont, Yankowsky later attended the Southern Alberta Institute of Technology (SAIT), qualifying as a power engineer. From 1970 to 1987 he worked for Edmonton power. Julius E. Yankowsky was returned as the Liberal member for Edmonton in 1993. However, he crossed the floor of the Chamber on December 9, 1994 and joined the Conservative government. In 1997 he was re-elected as the Tory member for Edmonton-Beverly-Clareview. Again, in 2002 he was the conservative member for Edmonton-Beverly-Clareview.

Source of information:

Canadian Parliamentary Guide (2002) p. 635

Young, Leslie G.

MEMBER OF THE LEGISLATURE 1971-1986

Born on August 19, 1934 in Compton Quebec, son of Gordon F. Young and Lena N. Cairns. Receiving his primary education in Hamilton, he later attended the University of Montreal, graduating in Arts and later receiving a Masters degree from the University of Massachusetts. From 1959 to 1962, he worked first as the editor of a journal and then as the manager of a farm radio forum. Young then worked for the Massachusetts government department of agriculture for three years. Coming to Alberta in 1965, he settled in Edmonton where he was employed by the Alberta School Trustee Association as an economic research consultant for five years. Young then became a businessman, economist, and business consultant. Interested in provincial politics, Les Young, running as a P.C., successfully contested Edmonton-Jasper Place in 1971. He was re-elected in 1975,1979,1982, and again 1986. Premier

Lougheed appointed Les Young as Minister of Labor in 1979. Young held the portfolio for seven years. Premier Getty later appointed Les Young Minister of Technology, Research, and Telecommunication in May 1986. Young rein finally ended when he was defeated in the 1989 Alberta election. By 1994, he was Alberta's commissioner in Hong Kong.

Source of information:

Canadian Parliamentary Guide (1972) p. 504

Younie, John

MEMBER OF THE LEGISLATURE: 1986-1989

Born March 3, 1950 in Olds, Alberta, son of Norman Younie and Myrtle Williams. Educated first at Red Deer College, Younie later attended the University of Lethbridge, graduating in Education in 1972. He became a schoolteacher in Ardrossan. Active in politics, Younie unsuccessfully ran as a New Democrat in the Rocky Mountain House constituency in 1979 and in the Edmonton Belmont constituency in 1982. He also failed in his attempt to win a seat in the House of Commons in 1984. Edward John Younie was returned as the New Democrat member for the Edmonton Glengarry constituency in 1986. He sat in the Legislature for three years as the N.D. environment critics. In 1989, he was defeated by Alberta Liberal leader John Decore and retired from politics. He is a Unitarian.

Source of information:

Canadian Parliamentary Guide (1988) p. 723

Yurko, William

MEMBER OF THE LEGISLATURE 1969-1979

MEMBER OF PARLIAMENT 1979-I984

Born on February 11, 1926 in Hairy Hill, Alberta, son of John N. Yurko and Helen Hanca. Educated in Red Deer, he later attended the University of Alberta, graduating with a degree in Engineering. Yurko also attended the University of Michigan and became an Edmonton petrochemical engineer. William J. Yurko was returned as the Progressive Conservative member for the Strathcona East constituency in the February 10, 1969 by-election and sat in the Legislature for ten years. Premier Lougheed appointed Yurko Minister of the Environment in 1971. Four years later he was transferred to the Public Works portfolio. In 1979 he did not seek re-election and retired from provincial politics in order to enter federal politics. William J. Yurko was returned the Progressive Conservative Member for the federal Edmonton-East riding in 1979. He sat in the House of Commons for five years. However, Yurko had a contested exchange with the P. C. Caucus and subsequently sat as an Independent. In 1984 Yurko, running as an Independent, failed in his bid to retain his seat. He placed fourth in a field of seven candidates. Later, he was the Chairman of the Alberta Oil Sands Technology Research Authority. By 1991 he was living in Edmonton. Yurko was a Baptist and in 1947 married Mary Paul of Edmonton.

Source of information:

Canadian Parliamentary Guide (1978)

Canadian Parliamentary Guide (1983)

Canadian Parliamentary Guide (1972) p. 504

Zariwny, Al

MEMBER OF THE LEGISLATURE 1993-1997

Born on February 3, 1944 in Thorhild, Alberta, son of Nicholas

Zariwny and his wife, Frances. He is of ethnic Ukrainian descent. Primarily educated in Thorhild, Zariwny later attended the University of Alberta, graduating over the course of time with an Arts degree, a Master's degree, and finally, a degree in law. Zariwny became a teacher in 1964 and two years later a principal. He later served as the secretary of the executive council, government of the Northwest Territories. In the early 1990's he became an Edmonton lawyer and businessman. Zariwny was admitted to the Alberta Bar in 1989 and to the Northwest Territories Bar in 1991. He is married to Anastasia Lewycky and they have two daughters together. Al R. Zariwny was returned as the Liberal Member for Edmonton Strathcona in 1993. He sat in the Legislature as a private member on the Opposition side of the Chamber. In 1997 he did not seek re-election, but returned to his Edmonton law practice.

Source of information:

Canadian Parliamentary Guide (1997)

Zwozdesky, Gene

MEMBER OF THE LEGISLATURE 1993-

Born in 1948. He attended the University of Alberta, graduating first in Arts and then in Education. He later became an Edmonton teacher. Gene Zwozdesky was returned as the Liberal Member for Edmonton Avonmore in 1993 and sat as a private member on the opposition side of the Chamber for four years.

Source of information:

Canadian Parliamentary Guide (1993-1997)

APPENDIX I: EDMONTON MEMBERS OF THE LEGISLATURE

Election Returns by City Constituency 1905-1955

*Where applicable, bolded names indicate the elected candidate

Constituency	Year	Candidate	Party
Edmonton			
	9-11-1905	Charles W. Cross	L
		William A. Griesback	C
	22-3-1909	**Charles W. Cross**	L
2 member constituency		**John A. McDougal**	C
		Albert F. Ewing	C
		John Galbraith	I
	27-5-1912	Charles W. Cross	L
	By-election	Albert F. Ewing	C
		Joseph R. Knight	SOC
	17-4-1913	**Charles W. Cross**	L
2 member constituency		**Albert F. Ewing**	C
		Alexander G. Mackay	L
		William A. Griesbach	C
		James D. Blayney	I
Edmonton East			
	7-6-1917	James Ramsey	C
		Frederick Duncan	L
		Joseph A. Clarke	I
		Sydney R. Keeling	SOC

Edmonton South

	17-4-1913	Herbert H. Crawford	C
		Alexander C. Rutherford	L
	7-6-1917	Herbert H. Crawford	C

Edmonton West

	7-6-1917	Albert F. Ewing	C

Constituency	**Year**	**Candidate**	**Party**
Edmonton, Multi-Member			
	18-7-1921	Andrew R. McLennan	L
5 member constituency		John C. Bowen	L
		Nellie L. M. McClung	L
		John R. Boyle	L
		Jeremiah W. Heffernan	L
		William J. Jackman	UFA
	27-10-1924	William T. Henry	L
	By-election	Albert F. Ewing	C
	28-6-1926	Final Count	
5 member constituency		John F. Lymburn	UFA
		Charles Y. Weaver	C
		Charles L. Gibb	B
		Warren W. Prevey	L
		David M. Duggan	C
	19-6-1930	Final Count	
6 member constituency		John F. Lymburn	UFA
		David M. Duggan	C
		Charles L. Gibbs	LAB
		William R. Howson	L

	Charles Y. Weaver	C
	William A. Atkinson	C
9-1-1931 By-election	Frederick C. Jamieson (*info not obtained)	C
22-8-1935 6 member constituency	Final Count	
	William R. Howson	L
	S.A. Gordon Barnes	SC
	David M. Duggan	C
	David B. Mullen	SC
	Gerald O'Connor	L
22-6-1936 By-election	Walter Morrish	L
	Margaret T.F. Crang	I
	Harry D. Ainley	CCF
7-10-1937 By-election	E. Leslie Gray (*info not obtained)	L

1940 5 member const.	Ernest C. Manning	SC
	J. Percy Page	I
	Hugh J. MacDonald	I
	Gerald O' Connor	I
	David M. Duggan	I
	Laurence Y. Cairns	I
	Elmer E. Roper	CCF
	Harry D. Ainley	CCF
	Charles Gould	SC
	Elisha East	SC
	James A. MacPherson	COMM
	N0D11an B. James	SC
	Charles B. William	SC
	Marjorie Pardee	I
	William H. Miller	CCF
	G. Francis Hustler	I
	S. A. Gordon Barnes	I
	John H. Green	I
	Final count	
	Ernest C. Manning	SC
	J. Percy Page	I
	Norman B. James	SC
	David M. Duggan	I
	Hugh J. Macdonald	I
22-9-1942	Elmer E. Roper	CCF
By-election		
	William Griffin	I
	Nelles V. Buchanan	L
5 member constit.	Final Count	
	Ernest C. Manning	SC
	Elmer E. Roper	CCF
	J. Percy Page	I

	William J. Williams	VET
	Norman B. James	SC
17-8-1948		
5 member const.	Final Count	
	Elmer E. Roper	CCF
	Louis W. Heard	SC
	Ernest C. Manning	SC
	J. Harper Prowse	L
	Clayton Adams	SC
5-8-1952		
7 member const.	Final Count	
	Ernest C. Manning	SC
	J. Harper Prowse	L
	Elmer E. Roper	CCF
	J. Donovan Ross	SC
	Edgar H. Gerhart	SC
	J. Percy Page	P.C.
	Harold E. Tanner	L
29-6-1955		
7 member const.	Final Count	
	Ernest C. Manning	SC
	J. Harper Prowse	L
	Abe W. Miller	L
	Harold E. Tanner	L
	J. Donovan Ross	SC
	J. Percy Page	P.C.
	Edgar H. Gerhart	SC

**One Member Constituency adopted for the 1959 General Election in the Urban Edmonton area.

APPENDIX II: CHRONOLOGICAL LIST OF ALBERTA LIEUTENANT GOVERNORS

Analysis by profession

Year of Appointment	**Name**	**Profession**
1905	G. H. V. Bulyea	Undertaker/ Politician
1915	R. G. Brett	Physician/Politician
1925	W. Egbert	Physician
1931	W. L. Walsh	Judge
1936	P.C.H. Primrose	Magistrate
1938	J.C. Bowen	Minister/Politician
1950	J.J. Bowlen	Rancher/Politician
1959	J.P. Page	Instructor/Politician
1966	J.W.G. MacEwan	Professor/Politician
1974	R.G. Steinhauer	Farmer
1979	F. Lynch-Staunton	Rancher
1985	W.H. Hunley	Businesswoman/ Politician
1991	T.G. Towers	Farmer/Politician
1996	H.A. 'Bud' Olson	Senator/Politician
1998	Lois E. Hole	Businesswoman/ Gardener

Membership of the Alberta Legislature Following General Elections:

1st	1905	25
2nd	1909	41
3rd	1913	56
4th	1917	60
5th	1921	61
6th	1926	61
7th	1930	63
8th	1935	63
9th	1940	57
10th	1944	60
11th	1948	57
12th	1952	60
13th	1955	61
14th	1959	65
15th	1963	63
16th	1967	65
17th	1971	75
18th	1975	75
19th	1979	79
20th	1982	79
21st	1986	83
22nd	1989	83
23rd	1993	83
24th	1997	83
25th	2001	83

Alberta Political Parties:

Name	Abbreviation	Year Founded
Liberal	L	1905
Conservative	C	1905
Progressive Cons.	PC	1942
Non-Partisan League	NPL	1917
United Farmers Alta.	UFA	1920
Reconstructionist	RECON	1935
Social Credit	SC	1935
Labor	LAB	1909
Socialist	SOC	1905
Communist	COMM	1920
Labor Progressive	LPP	1942
Co-op Commonwealth	CCF	1935
New Democratic Party	NDP	1962
Unity	UNIT	1937
Coalition	COAL	1955
Independent	I	1905

Province of Alberta Legislative Assembly (Leaders of the Opposition in the Alberta Legislature):

Name	Constituency	Year
Albert J. Robertson	(High River)	1905
Richard B. Bennett	(Calgary)	1909
Edward Michener	(Red Deer)	1910
George Hoadley	(Okotoks)	1918
James Ramsey	(Edmonton East)	1920
Alfred F. Ewing	(Edmonton West)	1921
John R. Boyle	(Sturgeon)	1922
Charles R. Mitchell	(Bow Valley)	1924
John C. Bowen	(Edmonton)	1926
George H. Webster	(Calgary)	1926
William R. Howson	(Edmonton)	1930
E. Leslie Gray	(Edmonton)	1937
James H. Walker	(Warner)	1941
Alfred Speakman	(Red Deer)	1942
James C. Hahaffey	(Calgary)	1943
James H. Walker	(Warner)	1944
J. Percy Page	(Edmonton)	1944
J. Harper Prowse	(Edmonton)	1948
J. W. Grant MacEwan	(Calgary)	1958
No leader of the Opposition formally recognized		1959
Michael Maccagno	(Lac La Biche)	1963
E. Peter Loughheed	(Calgary West)	1967
Harry E. Strom	(Cypress)	1971
James D. Henderson	(Leduc/Wetaskiwin)	1972
Robert C. Clark	(Olds/Didsbury)	1975
Raymond A. Speaker	(Little Bow)	1980
W. Grant Notley	(Spirit/Fairview)	1982
Ray Martin	(Edmonton Norwood)	1985
Laurence Decore	(Edmonton Glengarry)	1989
Grant Mitchell	(Edmonton McClung)	1994
Nancy MacBeth	(Edmonton Glenora)	1998
Kenneth Nicol	(Lethbridge East)	2001

Alberta Premiers 1905-2003:

Name	**Occupation**	**Year/Party**
Alexander Rutherford	Lawyer	1905/L
Arthur L. Sifton	Lawyer	1910/L
Charles Stewart	Farmer	1917/L
Herbert Greenfield	Farmer	1921/UFA
John E. Brownlee	Lawyer	1925/UFA
Richard E. Reid	Farmer	1934/UFA
William Aberhart	Teacher/Preacher	1935/SC
Ernest C. Manning	Preacher	1943/SC
Harry E. Strom	Farmer	1968/SC
E. Peter Lougheed	Lawyer	1971/PC
Donald R. Getty	Petroleum Executive	1985/PC
Ralph Klein	Journalist	1992/PC

The Speakers of the

Chamber:

Name	Constituency	Year
Charles W. Fisher	(Banff)	1905
Martin Woolf	(Cardston)	1920
Oran L.McPherson	(Little Bow)	1922
George N. Johnston	(Coronation)	1926
Nathan E. Tanner	(Cardston)	1936
Peter Dawson	(Little Bow)	1937
Arthur J. Dixon	(Calgary South East)	1964
Gerald J. Amerongen	(Edmonton Meadowlark)	1972
David J. Carter	(Calgary Egmont)	1986

Province of Alberta Legislative Assembly (The Lieutenant-Governors of Alberta in Order of their Appointment):

Name	Occupation	Year
George H. V. Bulyea	Merchant	1905
Robert G. Brett	Physician/MLA	1915
William Egbert	Physician	1925
William L. Walsh	Judge	1931
Philip C. H. Primrose	Magistrate	1936
John C. Bowen	Minister/MLA	1937
John J. Bowlen	Retired Rancher/MLA	1950
J. Percy Page	Retired Educator/MLA	1959
J. W. Grant MacEwan	Retired Professor/MLA	1966
Ralph G. Steinhauer	Farmer	1974
Frank C. L. Stauton	Rancher	1979
W. Helen Hunley	Business Woman/MLA	1985
T. Gordon Tower	Farmer/MP	1991
H. A. Olson	Farmer/MP/Senator	1996
Lois E. Hole	Philanthropist/Gardener	1999

About the Authors

Dr. Ernest G Mardon was born December 21, 1928, in Huston, Texas, the son of the late Professor Austin Mardon and Marie Dickey.

Educated in Gordonstoune, Schotland, he then attendent Trinity College, Dublin, before being called up for military service in teh Korean War as an officer with the Gordon Highlanders. He came to Canada in 1954 as bureau manager for United Press International, taught high school in Morinville and then did his Doctoral work in Medieval English at the University of Ottawa.

Among the first Faculty of the University of Lethbridge, Dr. Ernest Mardon was also a Visiting Professor at several other Canadian Universities. Dr. Ernest Mardon, *père* and Dr. Austin Mardon, *fils* have produced several works on Alberta political actors.

Dr. Austin Mardon was born on June 25, 1962 in Edmonton, the son of E.G. Mardon and May G Knowler, an Edmonton teacher. Educated at Lethbridge, he then did an M.A. at South Dakota State University and his Ph.D at Greenwish University, Australia. He then served as a research scientist and participated in a meteorite recovery expedition in the late 1980s spending some 50 days in a two-man tent, 10 miles from the South Pole. He is a life member of the New York Explorer's Club.

Dr. Mardon's main work ahs been his humanitarian efforts with those suffering from schizophrenia and other mental illness

The EDITOR

Mr. Justin Selner

Born December 11, 1990 in Edmonton, Alberta. Justin is a varsity swimmer for the University of Alberta, where he studies Honours Political Science.

www.ingramcontent.com/pod-product-compliance
Lightning Source LLC
La Vergne TN
LVHW091011080826
845145LV00003B/1230